when

he

doesn't

believe

when he doesn't believe

HELP *and* ENCOURAGEMENT
for WOMEN WHO FEEL ALONE *in* THEIR FAITH

nancy kennedy

WATERBROOK
PRESS

WHEN HE DOESN'T BELIEVE
PUBLISHED BY WATERBROOK PRESS
12265 Oracle Boulevard, Suite 200
Colorado Springs, Colorado 80921

Some of the stories in this book are composites of several different situations; details and names have been changed to protect identities.

ISBN 978-1-57856-434-7

Published in association with the literary agency of Ann Spangler and Company, 1420 Pontiac Road S.E., Grand Rapids, MI 49506.

Published in the United States by WaterBrook Multnomah, an imprint of the Crown Publishing Group, a division of Random House Inc., New York.

Library of Congress Cataloging-in-Publication Data
Kennedy, Nancy, 1954–
    When he doesn't believe : help and encouragement for women who feel alone in their faith / Nancy Kennedy.—1st ed.
        p. cm.
    Includes bibliographical references.
    ISBN 1-57856-434-4
    1. Wives—Religious life. 2. Marriage—Religious aspects—Christianity. 3. Husbands—Religious life.
4. Non church-affiliated people—Family relationships. I. Title: When he does not believe. II. Title.

BV4528.15 .K46 2001
248.8'435—dc21

                                                                                  2001026274

Printed in the United States of America
2009

10 9 8

*This book is dedicated to all those who keep
an empty space beside them in the pew
waiting for "that day."*

contents

acknowledgments

This, my sixth book, is in many ways the hardest book I will ever write. Because of that, I owe a debt of gratitude to all who have held my hand, pushed me when I needed it, refused to put up with my whining and excuses, advised and counseled me, spurred me on, corrected my errors, and told me I was: wonderful/brilliant/too full of myself/wrong, wrong, *wrong*.

In no particular order, I offer thanks to:

- Ann Spangler, my agent, who presented me with the idea for this book in the first place.

- Carol Hurley, just because.

- Mary Ann Fulkerson, an anchor during tough times and the one who knows my deepest, darkest secrets and loves me anyway.

- Jim Cole, my personal theology fact-checker and favorite Bible teacher and tamale eater. (Jim, you can bill me for your services later.)

- Ron Brown and Brian Proffit, the pastors-slash-friends I call on when my life doesn't work.

- Ray Cortese, not only my pastor and friend at Seven Rivers Presbyterian Church in Lecanto, Florida, but also my cheerleader.

- Phyllis Gorski, for always asking about Barry and for her encouragement.

- The folks at WaterBrook Press: Traci Mullins and Erin Healy, two *great* editors; Dan Rich and Rebecca Price for taking one more chance on me; all the enthusiastic sales reps and media people; plus all the others who make up such a terrific team. May God give you everlasting cookies.

- Jim "Walter Einstein" Nichols, my truly weird, grammar-grappling friend and the one who has weaned me away from using too many italics. *Thanks.*

- The Christian Writers Group e-mail list: 200+ of the neatest folks in cyberspace.

- Martin Luther, for his radical ideas about the just living by faith.

- Barry Kennedy, my best friend. What a ride it's been so far, Bear. No regrets.

- Finally, to the One who saw me from afar, set his love on me, and declared me "beloved." No words could ever express my gratitude, my God, my Savior, my Redeemer, and my Friend. I offer this book to you, not in repayment, but as a token of my worship. Amen.

And who knows but that you have come to royal position for such a time as this?

ESTHER 4:14

Introduction

I knew I shouldn't have said it the moment I opened my mouth. No, *before* I opened it—way before I opened it. But...I did it anyway.

I'd made a huge pan of lasagna, garlic bread, and my husband's favorite Italian sausages and sautéed onions. I even put radishes in the salad, just because I knew Barry liked them. Then I waited until he had taken a few bites. If it was true about a man's stomach being the way to his heart, I wanted to make sure I had a four-lane highway before I popped the question:

"Honey, will you come to church with us on Sunday?"

It's not that it was an unreasonable question. Another time it might even have been the right question. But not then. And I knew it. Just the day before he had told me he'd noticed how I had reprogrammed his truck's radio buttons to the Christian stations. Somehow he didn't appreciate it as much as I had hoped.

As for my invitation to church, he didn't say no, but he didn't say yes either. He said, "We'll see."

I sat there and stewed. *"We'll see"? What kind of an answer is that? If he means no, why doesn't he just say no?*

I picked at my dinner and tried to force a cheerful conversation about that night's hockey game on TV. I hate hockey! But even more, I hate getting myself stuck inside these pits.

A pit of disappointment.

A pit of impatience.

A pit of loneliness and discontent, frustration and fear.

The good news is, my times in the pits are rare these days. Most days I wake up, look over at my beloved husband, and know without a doubt that this man, this marriage, this life of being spiritually unequal for the past two decades have all been designed for me by the hands of a loving God. In many ways I consider my situation a gift.

Would I have chosen it? Hmmmm…that's a hard question. Can I plead the fifth on that?

Seriously, if any of us were able to see into the future, we would probably choose a husband who prayed with us daily, who led us spiritually, who woke up eager for church on Sunday mornings. (While we're at it, I'd like to add to the list a husband who didn't roll his dirty socks into balls and hide them behind the couch, who liked watching "chick flicks," and who didn't buy me enormous chocolate cakes for every holiday.)

However, knowing the future is not an option to us.

When Barry and I met and married more than twenty-five years ago, neither of us was a Christian. Three years into the marriage God called me into a relationship with himself through faith in Christ, and I responded with my whole heart. He gave me the gift of salvation and, along with it, the gift of this spiritually unequal marital yoke.

Of course, I didn't always see it as a gift. It took a few years of whining and complaining about my woeful lot in life to anyone who would listen before I recognized that it wasn't my circumstances that landed me in the pit but my attitude. That's when I heeded the First Rule of Pits: When you're in one, stop digging.

The Second Rule is mine: Throw away your shovel, dry your eyes, blow your nose, look up, and rejoice. Or as the psalmist put it,

> Praise the LORD, O my soul;
>> all my inmost being, praise his holy name.
> Praise the LORD, O my soul,
>> and forget not all his benefits—
> who forgives all your sins
>> and heals all your diseases,
> *who redeems your life from the pit*
>> *and crowns you with love and compassion,*
> *who satisfies your desires with good things*
>> *so that your youth is renewed like the eagle's.*
> (Psalm 103:1-5, emphasis mine)

Here's how I see it. God knows what circumstances I need that will (a) bring him glory, (b) advance his kingdom, and (c) transform me into the image of Christ. In his wisdom and sovereignty, this is his plan for me, my husband, our children, friends, family, community, and beyond. It's that far-reaching.

Does that mean it's easy? No, but following Christ rarely is. However, it's not impossible. God has promised he will give us everything we need to live lives of godliness and contentment. He redeems our lives from the pits, even the ones we dig for ourselves. He sets us high upon a Rock and gives us a reason to rejoice.

Even if our mates don't share our faith.

I realize not every unequally yoked marriage began as mine did.

Perhaps you married someone thinking he was a true believing Christian, only to discover he never was. Or you married a true believer, only to watch him backslide into sin. Either way, I imagine you feel as if you've been duped. Like the old bait-and-switch routine. You think you're getting one product and end up with another. Or it's as if someone played a mean trick on you. That's how Ginny,* an e-mail friend, describes her situation.

Ginny and Tom met and married while attending the same Christian college. They belonged to the same church, participated together in outreach activities, and prayed together every chance they could. "It just seemed natural that we would continue doing the same things after we got married," she wrote.

But they didn't. Almost immediately Ginny noticed that Tom didn't have any type of personal devotional life, and he often commented that memorizing Scripture was a "waste of time and mental faculties." Ginny chalked it up to a low point in Tom's spiritual life and hoped he would eventually come around.

After eight years of marriage, he still hasn't. In fact, Ginny says he has stopped everything: attending church and church functions, even praying before meals. He says he wants nothing to do with church and is so disappointed in God that he doesn't even believe there is a God anymore. Tom is angry and critical. And Ginny is…confused. She wonders, *Did I do something wrong? Is God punishing me? Why did this happen? This isn't what I signed up for. What could I have done to prevent it?*

In a recent e-mail Ginny wrote, "Our relationship may not withstand this test. It's not because I love him any less now that he no longer considers himself a Christian. I probably love him more—out of compassion for his wandering and lostness. Nothing is said between us about

---

* Because of the personal nature of this book, all names (except Barry's and mine) have been changed.

spiritual matters. As far as Tom's concerned, it's a closed subject. So I just wait and pray."

While on her wedding day Ginny never dreamed she would find herself living a spiritually unequal life with her husband, Briana knew exactly what she was getting into when she married Clint. Having grown up in a Christian home, Briana gave her heart to Jesus as a young girl. She met Clint, who was not a Christian, while in high school. They started dating, Briana got pregnant at age sixteen, and they got married.

Throughout the past seventeen years of their marriage—one that Briana describes as happy—Clint has encouraged Briana to attend church and even raise their two sons in the faith. He even occasionally joins the family at a church service, but that's as far as he's willing to go.

"It's my fault I'm in this situation," Briana says of her spiritually unequal marriage. "I'm paying for my sin, and I know it, so I really have no right to complain." She says she often feels guilty for wanting Clint to become a Christian, as if she somehow doesn't deserve it. Still…she hopes that someday God will answer her prayers for a spiritually equal marriage.

As we all do.

It's not selfish to desire our husbands' salvation. That's why we pray. We long for them to know the smile of God on their lives and to be at peace with their Creator. That's where our struggle lies. We want our experience to be theirs—and we want it soon. But unless the Spirit draws a person, even our best efforts are in vain.

Still, God hasn't forgotten us. He hears our prayers.

I don't know your situation or the degree of your difficulty, but if you're anything like these and other women I've talked to over the years—if you're anything like me—I know you sometimes feel as if you can't go on. You drive yourself crazy with what-ifs. You worry about the effect your spiritually unequal marriage will have on your children. You fret and feel guilty because you're certain everything is your fault.

You wonder if God will ever answer your prayers or if he even hears them.

You search the bookshelves looking for hope, maybe a five-step plan or seven secrets to loving your husband into the faith. You think, *If only I could find the key, if only I could change, if only I could be that perfect Christian wife, then surely my husband would fall on his knees before the Lord. Then we'd live happily ever after.*

Friend, it doesn't work that way. Plain and simple, your husband's relationship with the Lord isn't dependent on you. While God may use you in great ways as an influence, ultimately it's the Holy Spirit's job to change hearts. So relax! God's on his throne. Didn't Jesus himself say a sparrow doesn't fall to the ground without the Father's knowledge? No matter what your situation is, no matter how you arrived, keep in mind that God's promises to work out all things for your good and to prosper you spiritually are yours.

I've written this book to encourage you. To let you know that our God is a God of hope and power and strength. A God who sees, a God who knows. A God who hears the cries of the lonely, the confused, the brokenhearted. A God who brings laughter and song to the ones he loves and calls his own.

A God who has designed this life for you because he loves you.

Within these pages I pray you will find what you need, not only to survive or muddle through your marriage, but to thrive. To soar on eagle's wings and dance through the clouds, at least while doing the laundry. I've included stories from other women as well as my own stories—lots of practical advice and shared wisdom.

I've also included discussion-provoking questions at the end of each chapter to get you into the Scriptures. After all, the only wisdom and guidance we can completely trust and count on is the Word of God. Use these questions with a prayer partner or in a small group. Search God's Word together. You'll be glad you did.

One more thing: I'll be praying for you. I don't know your name, but I know your heart. So does God.

"Now to him who is able to do immeasurably more than all we ask or imagine, according to his power that is at work within us, to him be glory.... Amen" (Ephesians 3:20-21).

One

God Doesn't
Make Mistakes

*I*t was Easter Sunday, just this past year. As I took my usual place on the front row (center section, one chair over from the aisle), it struck me: I had come to church unmatched.

My daughter Laura was with me, and so was her boyfriend. They matched. Everyone else around me matched, at least I assumed they did. They looked as if they did. But I didn't.

There I was, sitting on the front row for all to see...wearing one black shoe and one blue shoe. *They weren't even the same style.* One black, one blue. Unmatched. Unequal. A pair, but not a pair.

At that moment I wanted desperately to be a real pair, just like everybody else. Two perfectly matching, size 7, black midheel pumps, not only matching each other, but complementing my black slacks as well.

The prelude music started: "All Hail the Power of Jesus' Name." Meanwhile, I sat fretting over my shoes. *Where was God when I made my choice?* I wondered. *Why would he allow such an obvious error? Didn't he know?* (Of course he did.) *Couldn't he have stopped me? Or supernaturally guide me to choose the one that matched?* (Of course he could have.)

Why didn't he?

Throughout the soloist's singing "I've Just Seen Jesus," throughout the choral reading when we were all asked to stand, throughout the worship chorus "Sing Hallelujah to the Lord," all I could think about was how unmatched I felt—and how powerless I was to change it. No amount of wishing it away could erase my choice. God had allowed me to go to church wearing a mismatched pair of shoes, and only a miracle from him could change it.

How Did We Get Here?

I've told this story hundreds of times before: My husband and I met, married, and fell in love—in that order. I'd left my home in California at age nineteen, an old maid in search of a husband. My brother had joined the navy, and the thought of sailors appealed to me. Unfortunately, or fortunately, depending on your point of view, on the day I went to visit the navy recruiter, he was out to lunch. However, the air force guy was in, and he was cute. So I sat down and signed up.

At the time, I was basically clueless. I'd goofed off in school and managed to graduate without any marketable skills or even a goal in life, other than finding a husband, that is.

Barry, a native New Yorker from Long Island, had joined the air force a year earlier, not to find a wife, but to find direction. Both stationed at Loring AFB, Maine, we met on the job at the base supply warehouse. He worked in the receiving department; I worked in the office where the receiving documents were filed.

What a coincidence.

I don't remember if I liked Barry right away or not. He didn't say much to me, although he visited my office just about once an hour to talk baseball with my supervisor. He'd say hello to me, but that was it.

I had heard through the rumor mill that he thought I was cute. Still, he didn't let me know, so I determined that he needed help asking me out. For a week or so I kept a nightly vigil in the chow hall, reading and drinking awful-tasting coffee. All my efforts only produced a sour stomach and jittery nerves.

Finally, I enlisted the aid of one of the civil service workers in his shop, who let Barry know that I was both interested and available. I left out "desperate"—didn't want to scare the poor guy off.

I liked the flattened baseball cap he wore (he rolled over it with a ton-and-a-half truck one day in the warehouse) and the crinkly smile lines around his brown eyes. And arm muscles to die for.

He eventually got the hint and asked me out—then stood me up on our first date. On our second date he invited me to go ice skating with him and bought me a pair of ice skates.

Since no man had ever bought me ice skates before (and because by then, at age twenty, I was an even older maid), several weeks after our skating date I asked him to marry me. Probably because no woman had ever proposed to him before (and therefore not realizing he could say no), he said yes.

Three months after that, wearing a navy blue pantsuit and sporting a giant pimple on my chin, I stood before a justice of the peace in Limestone, Maine, and vowed to love, honor, and cherish "till death do us part" some guy in a maroon sports coat whom I hardly knew and wasn't sure I loved.

Beyond his fascination with my then-red hair and green eyes, I didn't even have a clue how he felt about me either. At least we had a mutual ignorance in common. That and a great physical chemistry together, if you get my drift. As for shared interests...his main passion back then was baseball, softball, football, and ice hockey, while mine wasn't. I didn't really have any interests. All I knew was that nights were incredibly cold and lonely in northern Maine, and if nothing else, marriage guaranteed a date on Friday and Saturday nights. If it didn't work out...*oh, well.*

We were a long way from the Garden of Eden where the Lord God presented Adam with a "suitable helper" as a wife to be co-rulers over creation, walking together with God through the garden in the cool of the evening. Although we had each been raised in the same mainline denomination as children, neither one of us knew or cared anything about the Bible, Jesus, eternal life, or the kingdom of God.

That suited us just fine.

Another Proposal

I had made a vow to stay married to Barry until death parted us, but I don't think I meant it. Barry was a nice guy and all, but we had nothing in common. We liked eating lobster together on a Friday night and we liked sex, but that was about it. Not much to build a marriage on. Besides, he didn't fill the hole, the emptiness, the whatever it was that was missing inside. I had a feeling I wasn't meeting his needs either.

It wasn't his fault; I just wanted more. Something different. I thought daily, hourly about leaving, and I almost did, too—until I found out I was pregnant. Not wanting to split up our family, I stayed. I stayed on the outside, but I strayed on the inside, still looking for...something. Anything. I just didn't know what.

After the birth of our daughter, Alison, we decided she should be baptized. Not that we were getting religious all of a sudden, it just was the right thing to do.

So we did.

I think it was about that time I realized someone was pursuing me. I wasn't sure—I had been the aggressor in almost all my past relationships and didn't know what it was to be courted. To be wooed.

I liked it. I hated it. It was disconcerting and strange, yet at the same time, compelling. Someone wanted me.

Late at night I'd sneak out of bed and sit in the living room to think things through. I didn't know much about my pursuer. As a child I pictured him as severe and distant, cruel and vengeful. But at age twenty-three, I saw him as a lover, a bridegroom, eager to satisfy the object of his desire—me!

Through a series of events too numerous to list, on May 30, 1978, I received a marriage proposal from the One who loved me. In the ladies' room of the supply warehouse at Loring AFB, Maine, with a woman named Rita as a witness, I faced the One who had been courting me secretly. Rita opened her Bible and shared the good news: that I was and still am a wretched sinner. That my sin had separated me from Almighty God and that I was his enemy because of it. That his love for his people—for me—compelled him to send his beloved Son to earth, to live the perfect life I never could, and to die the death I deserved to die.

His presence filled that tiny room as Jesus proposed: my life for his.

Rita read from Romans 10:13, "Everyone who calls on the name of the Lord will be saved." She asked me, "Is this what you want?"

I told her, "More than anything!"

In an instant I'd received a proposal and married another. I'd married Christ! The one I really wanted all along. We would be together forever, we'd laugh together, we'd love each other. He would teach, I would learn. He would lead, I would follow. It would be bliss…except for one tiny snag—and he was on the other side of the bathroom door making his way down the hall to my office.

"My Wife, the Jesus Freak"

I exited the ladies' room redeemed, reborn, and obnoxious beyond description. I was certain Barry would want to hear all about what had just occurred in the bathroom and would want his own bathroom conversion experience as well. I ran to catch up with him, grabbed his arm and shook him, my words tumbling out into one long, run-on sentence.

"Barry,you'llneverguesswhathappenedtomejustnow. I'vegivenmylife-toJesus—Ithinktheycallitbeingbornagain—wantmetotellyouallaboutit?"

I took a breath, and he stepped away from me. Then, looking at me as if I had just sprouted three heads, he bolted down the warehouse stairs—with me right behind him hollering about what had just happened to me, chasing him all around the warehouse. What a sight that must have been!

In an instant I had gone from someone who was morose and moody, who cried often and harbored guilty secrets of past and present sins and desires, to a giddy and slaphappy fool. A babbling maniac. I'd been touched by God to my deepest core and wanted to share it with anyone who would sit still and allow me to talk.

Unfortunately Barry had acquired a sudden case of restless leg syndrome. Over the next few days, anytime I tried to tell him how he, too, could be saved in the bathroom (or any room of his choice), he'd bolt. Find something to do or somewhere he needed to be and run.

Since I was quicker back then, I ran after him, offering to find Rita so she could read her Bible to him, too. It all made perfect sense. Any day God would woo and draw Barry into a relationship with him as he had drawn me, and we could serve him together. It would be grand and glorious—and fun.

Any minute Barry would realize it and fall on his knees. Any minute…

That happened well over twenty years ago. I've since asked Barry about those early days of my faith, and he describes them in two words: loony tunes. He says that at first he thought I'd had a psychological reaction to the stress of our life at the time. Our air force enlistment was up, and we faced moving to civilian life in Portland, Maine. He had a job waiting, but we didn't have a place to live. Plus, job-wise I didn't know what I wanted to do. He figured this "Jesus thing" was a temporary diversion that I'd snap out of.

He hoped like crazy I'd snap out of it.

Meanwhile, I hoped like crazy that he'd snap *into* it. I thought I could convince him, pray him into the faith, show him, prove it to him, draw him, woo him. So I begged and pleaded with him, cried over him. Of all the Christians I had known in the air force, albeit only a handful, all had believing spouses. I assumed that was God's way and that my spouse would follow suit any day.

In the next chapter I'll tell you all about my year of obnoxiousness as I wrestled with trying to bring about a conversion experience for Barry. For now, let me tell you that for an entire year I relentlessly used every trick and any form of manipulation I could drum up to get my husband into the kingdom of God.

Unanswered Questions

It was a chilly evening in May. I was coming up on my one-year anniversary with Christ as well as my fourth anniversary with Barry. That night we had gone to the pier at Old Orchard Beach to play air hockey and eat pizza. I remember sitting on a waist-high rock wall, looking out at the Atlantic Ocean, amazed at how much I had come to truly love my husband that past year. My eyes were opened to his heart of mercy for others and how seriously he takes his responsibilities as a provider.

I knew that for me to go from marrying him to keep from being an old maid to genuine love—well, God just had to be real and the gospel just had to be true to have changed me so radically. And I desperately wanted Barry to understand true, biblical faith, but he didn't. He just didn't.

Since we were having a rare moment of fun that night, as if we had called a spiritual truce, I gave it yet one more try to get him to believe. I don't remember what I said, but I remember he listened. I felt him soften.

Of course, it could've been the pizza and the fact that I had let him whup me at air hockey, but I thought at the time it went deeper than that. He listened to me talk about Jesus! I thought for certain this was it—The Moment. But it wasn't, and I felt as if God had set me up for disappointment *again.*

I couldn't understand why it was taking so long. Had the Lord made a mistake in putting me in this spiritually unequal situation? Was he punishing me for something? Did I not pray enough or pray the wrong words? What about my discomfort and my desire to be united in faith as a family—was he unaware? Didn't he know (or care) that our daughter needed a father who would model Christ before her as she grew up?

Although it had been nearly a year since my conversion, it hadn't occurred to me even once that God knew exactly what he was doing, and that he was, and is, 100 percent, completely in charge of the universe. Nothing escapes his knowledge; nothing happens that he hasn't ordained. It's mind-boggling. But if we understood how God can give us free will *and* still be in total charge of everything that happens, then we would be God.

And that's the whole point. He's God, and we're not.

Therefore, he knew from before I existed that I would arrive at this place, unequally yoked with a guy from Long Island, New York, and that for twenty-plus years so far we would remain unequal yet whole.

Not a surprise, not a mix-up that he needs to correct, but his perfect design for my life thus far.

He knew your circumstances too.

God Never Says "Oops"

No matter how you arrived at this place of being spiritually unequal with your husband, one thing is certain: It didn't take God by surprise. Not only that, each one of us is exactly where he wants us to be, married to the exact person he wants us married to, for his exact purposes and for his glory and our ultimate good.

Just ask Joseph.

If anyone had a right to wonder if God knew what he was doing, it was Joseph. Genesis 37-50 details the saga of this man's life. Thrown into a well by his jealous brothers and left to die. Sold into slavery, also by his brothers. While a slave in Egypt, although he gained favor with Potiphar, one of Pharaoh's officials, he ended up in prison after Potiphar's wife falsely accused him of molesting her. The poor guy stayed in prison for years.

However, the story has an amazing ending, with Joseph eventually gaining such favor with Pharaoh that Pharaoh made him second in command. Irony of ironies, the story concludes with Joseph's brothers having to come to him for mercy during a time of famine. When he finally confronted his brothers about what they had done to him years earlier, he told them, "You intended to harm me, but God intended it for good to accomplish what is now being done" (Genesis 50:20).

Was it an accident that Joseph ended up in the well, in slavery, falsely accused, and imprisoned? Throughout Joseph's entire story are these words: "The Lord was with him." The Lord was with him...and he prospered. The Lord was with him...and showed him kindness... granted him favor...gave him success. Because God purposefully placed Joseph in Egypt and prospered him even while in prison, Joseph eventually saved the entire nation of Israel from starving during a severe worldwide famine.

Nothing happens apart from God's sovereign hand. "In him [Christ] we were also chosen," wrote the apostle Paul to the Ephesians, "having been predestined *according to the plan of him who works out everything in conformity with the purpose of his will*" (Ephesians 1:11, emphasis mine).

God is in charge and able to do above all we ask or think. When we marry as unbelievers only to be surprised by his call to faith, God is able to reconcile us both to himself. When a believing spouse strays or we discover we had been fooled and deceived by thinking we married a true believer, God is able to woo him back. Even when we marry an unbeliever, with eyes wide open and in defiance of the Lord's clear command, God is still able to make ours a "marriage made in heaven." If something could happen apart from his sovereign direction, then he's not God. And if he's God, then he's in complete and utter control. He never says "Oops."

What to Do When Your Shoes Don't Match

I'd gone to church on Easter with unmatched shoes—and God had allowed it. He didn't stop me, nor did he supernaturally change the blue one to black when I asked him to once I noticed my predicament. So I sat in church, unmatched.

About a quarter of the way through the service it struck me that I had a choice: I could either be miserable throughout the rest of the service because of my shoes, or I could just accept my situation, which was out of my control anyway, and enjoy the service. Either way, I'd remain unmatched, at least for the rest of that service. Either way, God knew exactly what he was doing.

It was Easter. Jesus had risen from the dead. So as the choir sang, I made my choice and tapped my toes. I thought, *What do you do when your shoes don't match and God's in control? That's easy—you dance.*

THINK ON THESE THINGS

- **Think** about how you go through your day. If you believed God has everything—including your husband and your marriage—entirely, wholly, totally in his sovereign care, a loving, all-mighty God working everything together for good, how would your everyday life be different? How would that affect your thoughts, attitudes, and actions?

- **Study** the life of Joseph (Genesis 37–50) or Esther (Old Testament book of Esther). What evidence can you find of God's hand directing their lives? Now think about your life, past and present. List all the evidences of God's directive hand, especially concerning your marriage.

- **Apply** the following scriptures to any doubts you might have about the sovereignty of God:
  Genesis 50:19-20
  1 Samuel 17
  Isaiah 40:26
  Matthew 10:29-31

• **Consider** what author and pastor Chuck Swindoll says in *Counseling Insights:* "Believers have been placed as ambassadors of the Kingdom of God to the homes in which they live. Their assignment is to represent Jesus Christ. The believer is one of many avenues through which God is pursuing the unbelieving spouse. The Christian is caught up in a grand pursuit that takes his or her life off center stage and puts it where it belongs, backstage and waiting for the Director's bidding." How freeing to know that God is the one in charge and that we can trust him fully.

• "Even when we fail God, he is able to bring good out of the situation. He is the Redeemer! He is the Master of bringing beauty out of ashes. He still cares, he is still in control and he still does all things well in his time. That is providence."

—Dee Brestin, *A Woman's Journey Through Esther*

"If Only..."

*A*fter I had given my life to Christ, it took less than a month for unreality to set in. Before, when I was miserable and steeped in sin, I pretty much decided Barry was a decent guy, and if I kept enough wine in my system, his flaws wouldn't bother me. Since he liked a beer or two, ours was a mutual arrangement, and except for an occasional hangover, we got along fine.

Then Jesus came into my life and started cleaning it up. That's when *I* decided Barry's needed cleaning up too. I did, however, know enough not to bombard him all at once. I had a plan. I'd be subtle, covert. I'd turn him into the best Christian husband God ever created. That's the unreality part.

See, I had a picture, a dream, of how Barry could, would, and should be if he'd only stop being so stubborn and just surrender and get it over with. Get saved. Accept Christ. Whatever you want to call it, I knew if he'd just do it, our life would be so much easier, so much fun. Heaven on earth.

I had it all planned how it would happen. Because of my Godly

Influence, he would be so Convicted of His Sin that he would become like putty and ooze repentance and sincere faith all over the place. Saved from hell, our lives would be swell.

You know how it is.

A woman named Keri says she has several versions of a recurring daydream. In daydream #1 she's doing something godly and self-sacrificing for her husband, Tom, like cheerfully picking up his dirty socks while praying without ceasing. Then, like a gust of wind, Tom bursts through the front door, whistling a Fanny Crosby hymn and clutching a brand-new *Men's Devotional Bible* (the one she gave him for his birthday). In his other hand is a bouquet of red roses, which he holds out to her as he announces, "Your prayers have been answered—I've been born again. Let's go out for dinner!"

Then all through dinner (after they say grace together for the very first time), Tom goes over every delicious detail of how he had finally realized everything she had told him all along was right and true. And because she's so godly and pure and overcome with joy and good cheer, she stifles the urge to say, "I *told* you I was right" and simply grins until her cheeks ache.

Daydream #2 has her going to church alone, "as always." When she takes her usual, lonely, solitary seat, dabs her tears, and prays that her heart won't break waiting for the service to begin, she feels a tap on her shoulder. Thinking it's some "complete" family wanting her seat so they can all sit together, she looks up in annoyance…only to see Tom standing there all awkward and cute in his navy blue Dockers and white polo shirt with his hair freshly combed.

"Is this seat taken?" he asks. Speechless, she slides over to let him in, while the angels in heaven rejoice and the choir sings the "Hallelujah Chorus."

What wife of an unbeliever hasn't gone through a hundred versions of the same daydream? The details may differ, but the core message remains the same: If only my husband would give his life to Christ, life would be perfect. We would pray together all the time, search the Scriptures, and discuss dispensationalism, infant baptism, and the five points of Calvinism.

We would live in harmony, lie down in peace. Even our arguments would begin and end with prayer. We'd be fair to one another at all times and selflessly devoted. He would lead; I would gladly follow. He wouldn't eat spaghetti in bed at midnight—or snore.

Yes, life would be bliss. However, often our husbands don't share the same dream, at least not right away.

Don't Try This at Home

In the early days of my newfound faith, I was what you might call a raving lunatic. Since no one in either of our families was a born-again Christian, I didn't have anyone to model my life after. All I had was zeal and a desire for an ideal Christian marriage and family. So, filled with great expectations and armed with more enthusiasm than knowledge, I set out to win my husband to the Lord any and every way I knew how.

There's a bumper sticker that reads "Some people were created to serve as a warning to others." That best sums up my life. I win any contest for the Most Obnoxious Christian Wife, hands down.

But you know how it is. You want something so badly you can taste it. You have an ideal, a desire, in plain view. You know that if you could only make it happen, you could breathe again. You could relax, let down your guard. You could enjoy your life *finally.* You think:

> If only my husband were a Christian…
> He would remember I like coral roses

He would turn off the TV and talk to me
Take out the trash, lead me in prayer.

If only my husband were a Christian...
Our finances would improve
Our children would behave
Our sex life would be more satisfying.

If only my husband were a Christian...
He would stand up to his boss
And his mother
He would find some decent friends
Tuck in his shirt, lose weight, stop smoking, mow the lawn.
If only my husband were a Christian...
Life would be one joy-filled experience after another.

So you have all these wants and desires and expectations of what you think your life could be—should be—like...if only your husband were a Christian. You look around your church and imagine what life is like between Mr. Slightly-Balding-but-Awfully-Cute and his equally cute wife and even cuter kids whom you see every Sunday, all holding hands. You imagine their dinner conversation is regularly dotted with Scripture and they plan their vacations around Christian family life seminars. And because that's what you want from your marriage, you take these expectations home and announce them to your husband.

Even if you don't say a word.

I may be guilty of many things but never subtlety. Plus, when I want something, I'll find any way I can to get it—or die trying.

Although it pains me to admit this, I used to leave opened Bibles scattered around the house, with key passages highlighted and circled. There's nothing like Romans 3:23 ("All have sinned and fall short of the glory of God") on the back of the toilet, unless it's having every radio we owned conveniently set at Christian radio stations, or so I thought.

When we'd watch TV together, if Barry left the room, I'd switch the channel to Christian programming. When he'd return, I'd pretend I sat on the remote and it just happened to change. "Like a miracle," I'd tell him.

Once I invested in a case full of assorted gospel tracts—the scary, comic book kind—and I'd put one in his lunch several times a week. I'd sign a birthday or a thinking-of-you card with a scripture. I'd pray loudly and often in my room.

I even dragged our then-toddler Alison in on the act, teaching her to say on cue, "Daddy, go church?"

I'd make sure to leave a church bulletin on the front seat of Barry's work truck (just in case he was interested), and I interjected snippets from the pastor's sermon into as many conversations as I could. I guess I expected that all my efforts would pay off, that I could create The Moment. I mostly created a lot of hard feelings. Barry would brace himself whenever he'd sense a gospel ambush was about to occur. He'd say, "Gimme my wife back—Jesus-free!"

Then one day the tide turned. I'd been on a holy rampage, offering Barry all sorts of flimsy reasons that he should come to faith in Christ. ("It'll be good for your career," "We could go to family camp," "You could be in heaven with me someday.") I just wasn't hitting the right buttons. I'd been a Christian less than a few months and hadn't built up an arsenal. I was mostly lobbing makeshift cherry bombs.

At one point I tried pleading pathetically. Trust me, I can be extremely pathetic. *Please, Barry. Pleeeeeeeze. Our lives would be so much better if only you were a Christian.*

I'll never forget this one particular day. As we stood in the kitchen of our Portland, Maine, apartment, Barry looked at me for the longest time. I couldn't tell what he was thinking, only that I had finally touched something in him. "You really want a Christian husband that badly, don't you?"

The way he posed the question, I wasn't sure where he was going with it. Still, my heart pounded. Although I dared not raise my hopes, I couldn't help thinking maybe my hard work was about to pay off. This would be The Moment.

He continued calmly. "I'll tell you what. Next time you go to church, you pick out the Christian husband you want and marry him. I won't stand in your way."

Sadly, that wasn't the last time I pushed my husband to make that offer. Happily, it's been years since his last one.

Reality Bites

"'If only' thinking is a direct path to disappointment and a sure way of distancing you from your spouse," writes Greg Cynaumon in *Married but Feeling Alone,* the book he coauthored with his wife, Dana. "After awhile, the spouse on the receiving end of 'if only' thinking grows tired of always falling short in that mate's eyes. When we try to compare reality with 'if only,' we're playing the game of childhood wishing, only the stakes are much higher than [wishing for] a new bike or new doll."

After years of "if only" thinking, a friend's husband finally came to faith in Christ a few years ago. The circumstances were a dream come true for my friend. Rick had accompanied Marie to church one Sunday night, and as the pastor gave an altar call at the end of the service, Rick stepped forward.

Marie says she had been praying with her head bowed and eyes closed and didn't notice Rick had slipped out of his seat. It wasn't until she heard several gasps that she looked up and saw her husband praying with the pastor. She hurried to join him, taking with her all her expectations of what life would be like now that her prayers for Rick had finally been answered.

The other night, as we sat and ate ice cream together, Marie told me Rick is more at peace than he ever was before and is "frighteningly generous" with their money. However, life isn't the everlasting bliss she had dreamed it would be.

"He's still Rick," she said, "which is okay, except I really thought his personality would change. I expected him to be different—outgoing and vocal about his faith. It's there, he believes it and lives it, but he's quiet about it."

She said when Rick first came to faith, they read the Bible together every night, but once they finished Revelation, Rick said, "Well, I've read the Bible," and hasn't opened it since.

"I realize now that even though Rick's a Christian, God still wants me to turn to him as my Husband," she says.

Here's what other women say about reality with their Christian husbands:

> I am married to a strong Christian husband, and we pray together and occasionally do a Bible study together and have good spiritual discussions. However, I wish he were better at evangelism. Mostly I'm not good at it myself and I wish I had a husband who was able to speak freely about his faith to make up for my own lack. —Marcia

> I'm better off having a Christian man for a husband, but I doubt we'll ever see eye to eye about Bible studies and praying together more than just one little prayer at night. He loves Jesus as much as I do, but we serve him in different ways. None of us should ever think our husbands

should feel or act exactly the same as us. I think he should tithe and pray more, but I have left all that up to the Lord. My job is to be loving and faithful to him—and not nag!

—Jessica

I'm a pastor's wife, and it's a rare thing for us to sit down and have devotions together, although I'm praying one day we'll evolve into a couple who does that. Also, we have differing prayer habits, and that's been something I've had to accept. But we are growing, and the fact that it sometimes bothers me has been a matter of prayer itself.

—Debbie

I know I don't qualify as a wife, but I'll give you my point of view as a Christian husband: There is no "ideal" husband who will *never* quarrel, who will *always* agree, who will *always* do exactly the right thing by you and your children. The most you can hope for in this life is a husband who loves and respects you, and if a conversion and salvation experience makes him work at being a better man, yet he still falls short of her expectations, a wife should be grateful for whatever ground she gains.

—Carl Phillips, columnist

As Jo Berry writes in *Beloved Unbeliever,* "If Christian marriages were so glowingly wonderful, there wouldn't be so many lessons taught, sermons preached or books written on how to have a happy one. Christianity is not a panacea for all of our problems; it is a faith relationship with a God who is able to help us overcome sin."

Whenever I start indulging in "if only" fantasies, I just remind myself that Christianity hasn't made me a perpetual party to live with, nor am I the ideal Christian. So it's both unrealistic and unfair to place that expectation on an unbelieving mate.

What Then Can I Expect?

When it comes to expectations, first of all you can expect opposition, whether subtle or blatant, passive or purposeful. To your husband, the Bible might be foolish, church a waste of a good Sunday morning, and all Christians hypocrites. He might think Jesus is fine for women, children, and the elderly, but his priority is his job and putting food on the table or playing with model trains.

He may spit fire and breathe smoke at the mere mention of God, or he may encourage you to study, pray, and build relationships with your Christian friends, even listen to your insights on the pastor's sermon, yet not want it for himself and graciously dismiss any attempt to draw him to Christ.

As the apostle Paul explained, "The natural, nonspiritual man does not accept or welcome or admit into his heart the gifts and teachings and revelations of the Spirit of God, for they are folly (meaningless nonsense) to him; and he is incapable of knowing them (of progressively recognizing, understanding, and becoming better acquainted with them) because they are spiritually discerned and estimated and appreciated" (1 Corinthians 2:14, AMP).

In other words, expecting your unbelieving husband to understand spiritual things is unreasonable on your part. Especially if you are a new believer yourself and this is new to the both of you, more than anything else you can expect your husband to be confused and bewildered: *What happened to my wife?* Angry: *What do you mean you won't go drinking with me anymore? You too good all of a sudden?* Embarrassed: *My wife's a Jesus freak!* Scared: *How long is this going to last?*

If you expect opposition, then you won't be surprised when it comes. The danger, of course, is the temptation to place yourself in a constant state of spiritual defensiveness, always on alert for "enemy attacks." Yes, an unbeliever lacks spiritual discernment and is opposed to the truth of the gospel, but an obnoxious, defensive Christian is only inviting conflict.

A better way is to expect that your husband wants harmony between the two of you. Chances are he doesn't want to fight. He just wants his dinner on time and a warm, responsive body to curl up next to in bed. So expect opposition, but don't focus on it. Focus instead on what binds you together as a couple. What do you enjoy doing together? What are your shared (or potentially shared) interests? Is there something your husband has expressed an interest in that you can share?

Make a conscious effort to find common ground between the two of you, even if it's just that you both like your eggs cooked the same way. At least that's a start. Pray and ask the Lord to help you build a bridge to bring you closer to the one he's given you to love.

Expect your husband to appreciate that.

You can also expect God's blessings to fall on your husband because of the covenant relationship the Lord has with you. "For the unbelieving husband has been sanctified through his wife" (1 Corinthians 7:14). Because marriage binds a man and woman together as one flesh, when one of the partners is a believer, the blessings of God fall on the unbelieving mate as well. When God blesses me with peace and joy, when I'm blessed with a job I love, with wisdom to make decisions, with inner strength to deal with life's problems, it splashes over on my husband to enjoy as well. A satisfied, contented wife is a blessing from God even to an unbelieving husband.

God is for me, not against me. He is for my marriage and will give me all the resources I need to thrive in it.

I can expect that.

I can also expect that God can and will use my husband as his tool of blessing in my life. I vividly recall a situation as a new Christian. I needed a jacket, money was tight, and I wanted to show Barry that the Lord would provide one for me. I wanted him to see that God really was real and the Bible really was true. So I prayed for a jacket.

Shortly after that, Barry got a call for some overtime work, and the following payday he brought me home the jacket I had picked out at the store but couldn't afford to buy.

I had expected the Lord to provide, but I hadn't expected him to use my husband as his means. To be honest, I was ticked at God—I wanted a jacket to fall from the sky, or at least an envelope with money to miraculously appear under the mat on our doorstep. But knowing what we both needed, God blessed Barry so he could in turn bless me.

A woman married to an unbeliever can expect opposition as well as blessing, and from her marriage she can expect to reap what she sows.

If she sows a "me vs. you" mentality, defensiveness, and self-righteous judgmentalism...

If she expects to be miserable and considers her marriage a burden or "the cross I must bear"...

If she's discouraged and fretful...

Then she can expect her marriage to be exactly the hell on earth she makes it.

But if a woman sows a desire to find common ground with her husband and sows patient acceptance of him just as he is...

If she encourages, admires, and respects him and rejoices that God includes him in his covenant of grace with her...

And if she sows hopeful anticipation of what the Lord can and will do in both of their lives...

Then she can expect to reap a marriage filled with moments of happiness and joy. A woman can expect challenges and hard times and moments of loneliness and being misunderstood too, but not without the needed resources to get through them—as an individual child of the Almighty and as a couple set apart by his grace.

All in all, those are *great* expectations.

THINK ON THESE THINGS

- **Think** about and name some common expectations of marriage. Where do these ideas come from? What are/were some of your expectations for your marriage as it pertains to your unequal yoking?

- **Study** Psalm 62 and Acts 17:24-28. What do you think is the root cause of "if only" thinking? How do "if only" thoughts affect a woman's attitude toward her husband? For help in combating such thoughts, memorize 2 Corinthians 10:5 and Philippians 4:8.

- **Apply** the following scriptures to the subject of unmet expectations by meditating on them whenever your thoughts start to wander:
  Psalm 26:2-3
  Isaiah 26:3
  Romans 12:2
  Hebrews 3:1

- **Consider** these suggestions from Greg Cynaumon, author of *Married but Feeling Alone:* "The second you feel a bout of bitterness coming on over unmet expectations, pray for your partner and yourself. Pray to God for the strength to deal with the things within your control, while releasing those issues outside of your control.... Face it, the devil loves nothing more than to see us damaging our marriages by comparing our expectations to reality."

• "Often God has us surrender our dreams because our dreams are usually for *us*. God wants our dreams to be for *him*."
    —Stormie Omartian, *Just Enough Light for the Step I'm On*

Three

Feelings, Whoa, Whoa, Whoa, Feelings

*U*nlike the New York Yankees, whom former manager Yogi Berra described as having "deep depth," at age twenty, I was severely lacking in the depth department. While it was the ice skates Barry had bought me on our first date that prompted my marriage proposal to him, it was his car that clinched it for me.

He had just returned to Maine from a visit to his home in New York where he had picked up his car: a 1973 Mercury Comet, white with burnt orange trim and interior, three-speed, "high performance 302 V-8 engine." Definitely a hot car.

Although I wasn't sure how I felt about Barry, I loved his car the moment I saw it. I could see myself driving that thing, and I couldn't wait until Barry and I were "one" and the car would be legally mine.

Since Barry was only twenty-two and brimming with testosterone at the time—and I had shiny red hair—he, too, couldn't wait to teach his new wife to drive a stick shift. But just as my red hair was not natural, neither was my ability to perform anything requiring physical coordination. To put it mildly, I had trouble with the clutch/gas/brake pedals. I could do one at a time, but not two at once, unless you count the gas and brake pedal mishap.

I eventually learned how to get the car going forward, and I did okay as long as I didn't have to stop. Thankfully, I was cute back then and Barry was forgiving. But what I remember most about trying to drive the Comet were my feelings of utter frustration. Of wanting so badly to drive that stinkin' car, yet not being able to. I kept getting jerked around, literally. The harder I tried, the more the car seemed to fight against me. Just as I would get to a point where I thought I could handle things, I'd hit a patch of ice on the road or get stuck parked on a hill. I'd cry and scream, rant and rave. If I was out alone, I'd panic because I didn't have anyone around to help me. I was angry at Barry for buying such a stupid car in the first place. I felt helpless and hopeless and ticked off.

Eventually the car won, and I gave up driving it. The following year we traded it for a sensible, *automatic* Plymouth Duster. At least vehicularly, my life after that has been relatively jerk-free.

Emotional Whiplash

If you're the wife of an unbelieving husband, or if you're married to a believer who has strayed from the faith and is indifferent or even hostile to spiritual matters, you understand emotional whiplash. That feeling of being jerked around. As Penny from Indiana says, it's that feeling of being yanked every Sunday morning when you have to make a choice to get up and leave the man you love to go be with the Lord and the Christian family you love. You feel torn, and no matter what you decide—to go or stay—you feel guilty.

Or as Carolyn says: You sit in church and you know what you're hearing is soothing to your soul because it's the truth. You know this is where you belong, that this is your family. So you want to stay forever, but not just because you love being with like-minded Christians. You want to stay because you know you're going to have to "pay" when you get back home to your husband. For some, the price is dear—from quiet indifference to open hostility. You go from mountaintop to valley in a matter of minutes.

That's emotional whiplash.

More than any other emotion, loneliness tops the lists of most women in spiritually unequal marriages. A woman may feel connected with her husband through shared activities and interests, the two might share a satisfying sexual relationship, they may genuinely like each other, yet when it comes to the deepest, most important and vital aspect of her being— her relationship with God—she feels an impenetrable wall between them. And with that wall comes a loneliness so deep it's frightening.

So she goes to church to be with like-minded Christians with whom she can share her faith, but she's lonely there, too. She feels a connection, a sense of belonging with these people, yet there's a sense of incompleteness, of it somehow being not right. *If the two are supposed to be one flesh, then how can it be that I'm here alone? How can it be that the one I love most on earth doesn't share the most important part of my life?*

Joanne says, "After eighteen years, I've gotten used to the loneliness, but it's still never easy. Fortunately, my husband works on Sunday mornings, which takes away that excruciating choice of whether to go to church alone or stay home. We get home about the same time and then spend all Sunday afternoon together."

Even though that takes care of the surface issue—the logistics of attending church—she says there's still a wall of loneliness to contend with. She still gets in her car by herself every week.

Same with Kathy, who says, "Sometimes I'll be driving toward church, and I'll feel a pull on my heart. Sometimes I turn around and go home. I feel as if I just can't do it one more time alone."

Lisa says on her loneliest Sunday mornings she just tries to get to this one particular intersection. Then when she gets there, she tells herself, "No turning back" and reminds herself of the time some of Jesus' disciples turned back and no longer followed him. He asked his chosen twelve if they, too, wanted to desert. Peter answered for the bunch, "Lord, to whom shall we go? You have the words of eternal life" (John 6:68).

"But it still gets lonely," she says.

Friend, if and when you find yourself aching with loneliness, that's when you have an important choice to make: To whom will you go to ease your loneliness?

Listen to me carefully when I tell you: Guard your heart. God created women with a need to feel emotionally connected. Be warned: When there's a wall of loneliness in your marriage, don't be surprised when everywhere you turn you find godly, caring men who seem to be heaven-sent to meet those needs and ease your spiritual loneliness.

Guard your heart.

When that Christian man asks how you're doing and offers to counsel and pray with you and give you a man's perspective, no matter how pure his intentions, no matter how kind and sincere he is, don't make him your intimate confidant. Don't, don't, *don't.* Without meaning to, you will—you WILL—fall into a trap of emotional adultery.

Guard your heart. You don't have to be rude, just careful. No matter what you may tell yourself to justify developing a relationship with another man, even calling him a "brother" in Christ, a lonely heart isn't discerning. It only wants to be comforted.

And your heart belongs to only one.

God Is Enough

So what do you do with your loneliness? What do you do when you're the only one in your household who has been touched by the gospel and who understands the call to follow Jesus? What do you do when you're laughed at or ridiculed or rebuffed for your faith by the person who's supposed to be your soul mate?

What do you do when you tear yourself away on a Sunday morning and feel ripped in half for doing so? What do you do when you sit alone in the pew and either mentally or literally keep the space next to you open because that's where you picture your husband sitting? What do you do when you can't help but count all the complete couples around you? When your child tells you that her Sunday school teacher thinks you're a single mom? When you realize no one at church even knows what your husband looks like and you're so lonely in your faith that you think you can't go on?

When you find yourself in these lonely situations, what you do is thank God for his gift. In many ways, loneliness is God's gift to his people. If we were never lonely, we wouldn't know of our need. If we didn't have a need, we wouldn't know of God's sufficiency to meet it.

When I look back, sometimes I think I was better off in the early days of my faith, when the loneliness from being misunderstood was more acute. In those days, whenever I felt I couldn't bear it any longer, I'd retreat to the bathroom, fill the tub with hot water, hop in, and pray. I'd memorize verses from Psalms and tell them to myself over and over:

> Hear my cry, O God;
>> listen to my prayer.
> From the ends of the earth I call to you,
>> I call as my heart grows faint;

lead me to the rock that is higher than I.
(Psalm 61:1-2)

My soul finds rest in God alone....
    He is my mighty rock, my refuge....
    Pour out your hearts to him,
    for God is our refuge. (Psalm 62:1,7-8)

Praise be to God,
    who has not rejected my prayer
    or withheld his love from me! (Psalm 66:20)

    In faithfulness you have afflicted me.
May your unfailing love be my comfort. (Psalm 119:75-76)

Sometimes I'd take two or three baths a day. You could say, in my case, loneliness led to cleanliness. More important, it led me to the One, the only One, who could take my loneliness away.

These days I don't have a bathtub, but I do have a brown armchair. I call it my prayer chair, and in my mind it's the place where the Father sits. Nobody in my household knows this, but when I'm sitting in that brown chair with my legs draped over one arm and my head resting against the back, I'm really sitting on my Father's lap, exchanging my loneliness for his sufficiency and receiving his comfort.

I don't know how God does it, only that he does: He just shows up. He lets you know that he cares more than you can comprehend, that you will survive, even thrive. He reminds you that your Maker is your true husband (Isaiah 54:5), and he sits with you at church when you think you're there alone. He reminds you that you're never, ever alone and whispers, "I'm enough."

And he is.

Handling Those Other Pesky Emotions

Wouldn't it be nice to have all your feelings and emotions on a clipboard checklist where you could say, "Okay, I've dealt with loneliness, now let's go on to the rest"? Then *boom, boom, boom,* you could cross them off one at a time until you got to the end. Finally, once you had finished, you could get on with the business of living the joy-filled and abundant life you thought came with being in Christ.

As my teenage daughter says, "Get *real.*"

Real is having your emotions and feelings all jumbled and even contradictory. Real is emotional whiplash. Real is being with your Christian friends, relaxing and enjoying spiritual communion, maybe talking about "no condemnation in Christ" or an answer to a specific prayer. Your emotions rise. Your heart fills with wonder and worship.

But then you go home, and as you pull in the driveway, your good mood gets dashed. You wish you could experience that same communion with your husband as you do with your friends, and you're frustrated because it's taking so long. You're tired of waiting, angry because you have to miss out on events like couples' banquets and marriage retreats because your husband refuses to go to anything that sounds even vaguely Christian.

Maybe you begin to doubt whether this Christianity really is true—and you feel confused. Or maybe the thought grips you: What if my husband dies without Christ? So you start to worry. You're afraid, anxious. You're all these things and more. Not always all at once, but sometimes.

And you don't know what to do.

Although emotions don't come in a handy checklist, let's take them one at a time.

Frustration

If we're not careful, it's easy to forget that God's gift of salvation is *not* on a first-come, first-served basis. Unless we keep in mind that the Lord has his own timetable and plan for our families, whenever we hear of someone else's husband coming to faith, we may be tempted to explode in frustration. *But I've been waiting longer! I've been good! It's MY turn!*

Proverbs 13:12 gets it right when it says, "Hope deferred makes the heart sick." It makes you want to slam cupboards and kick doors. It doesn't help to have well-meaning friends tell you to be patient either. *You want patient? I'm so patient my eyeballs are popping out and I'm breathing smoke!*

One woman I talked to recalled the time she and her husband were having a great discussion. He was going on and on about what a good job she did with the kids and how proud he was of her.

"Normally I eat this stuff right up, but that time it pricked a nerve," she said. "All I could think about was how long I had been praying and waiting, and he was just standing there in the kitchen telling me how wonderful I am."

When she couldn't take any more, she said she grabbed her husband by the front of his shirt, pushed his six-foot frame against the wall and shouted, "Don't you see Christ in me?!"

"He assured me that, yes—when I wasn't shoving him against walls and pulling on his chest hair—that he did, indeed, see Christ in me. In fact, he tells everyone that I'm the 'world's best Christian.'"

When she eventually let him go, she asked him, "Then why aren't you a Christian too?"

The answer is, it's not about her or you or me. It's not about our Christian example, or even the number of years we wait or the volume of prayers we pray. It's not even about your husband and whether or not he sees Christ in you. It's about God's plan and his timing and how "no one can come to [Jesus] unless the Father...draws him" (John 6:44).

When frustrated and impatient, what we need most from God is confidence and trust in his sovereignty. Preferably before we grab our unsuspecting husbands by the shirt.

"Fussing doesn't get you what you want," writes Jeanne Zornes in her book *When I Prayed for Patience...God Let Me Have It!* "Fussing only reveals that we cannot accept the circumstances God has put us in. It is a symptom of an inner state of [the] soul that has not come to rest with God."

While patience comes through trials and irritations and all those opportunities God sends our way so that we might produce more of this fruit of the Spirit, confidence comes from a solid grasp of biblical theology. We can handle frustration if we're confident that:

- He who began a good work in us (and our families) will finish what he has started (Philippians 1:6).

- God knows those who are his, including those who will come to faith sometime in the future (2 Timothy 2:19), and that all who are his *will* come (John 10:16).

- God is not slow in keeping his promise and doesn't want anyone to perish (2 Peter 3:9). This doesn't guarantee anyone's salvation, but it shows a glimpse of the Father's heart.

- He has made everything beautiful *in his time* (Ecclesiastes 3:11).

- He is able to make all grace abound to me (2 Corinthians 9:8), including developing my patience when I want to quit and keeping me calm when I want to scream.

Anxiety, Fear, and Worry

Before coming to the place of resting and trusting in God's sovereignty, how many of us drive ourselves crazy with worry about our husbands' spiritual condition? *What if I say or do something wrong and it turns him away forever? What if I don't say or do the right things? What if I'm not a good example? What if he sees me sin?*

We fear the worst: *What if he gets in a horrible accident and dies without Jesus?* Patty says, "Every time my husband leaves to go anywhere, I study his face, certain it will be the last time I'll ever see him. *Ever.* Then when he drives away, I feel my stomach tense. I cry and stare out the window, pleading with God to save him right then. I don't think I can bear planning his funeral, although that's what I do in those hours he's away."

She says when she's not worrying about his imagined death, she worries that Jesus will come back too soon. Even when her husband is home, she still worries, plagued with "what ifs."

However, if you're crying in the kitchen—and you're not chopping onions—it's hard to explain to your very-much-alive husband that you're grieving his untimely, Christ-less death.

"Do not be anxious about anything" (Philippians 4:6), exhorted the apostle Paul. Easy to say, hard to do.

"Do not worry," says Jesus. "Who of you by worrying can add a single hour to [her] life?" (Matthew 6:25,27). Or her husband's life? Or who of you by worrying can bring your husband into the kingdom?

Just as I learned to deal with my impatience and frustration through trusting in God's grander plan and his perfect timing, so too I've dealt with my worry and fear through trusting in his loving sovereignty over my life as well as my husband's. When I know that not a single molecule in the universe escapes God's control, I know nothing will happen in my life by random chance or accident.

And no amount of worrying will change a thing.

Anger, Resentment, and Discontent

You can't help it, or so you think. On any given Sunday morning, while your husband remains a lump under the covers and you're getting yourself and your kids ready for church, you feel your teeth clench. Pretty soon you're fuming because he can't—or won't—see the need for a faith of his own. He's perfectly content to live his life the way he's always lived it and sees no need to change, thank you very much. Even if his life is going down the tubes, he doesn't see the need for "that religious stuff." He thinks you're an uptight, goody two shoes, Bible nut and says you'd be a whole lot happier (and easier to live with) if you'd just go back to the way things used to be.

But you know you can't go back...and you're angry. Maybe you think your husband's rejection of spiritual things is out of spite—he's doing it just to tick you off. Maybe that makes you close the closet door a little too hard when you're getting dressed for church (and accidentally wake him up). Maybe you glare at him as you tie your little one's shoes and let him know a "good father" would lead his family to church.

You start picking your husband apart. You hate his "worldly" habits and attitudes. You shake your head in disgust at his profanity or smoking or beer drinking and walk out of the room if he turns on anything other than Christian TV or radio. You start thinking of him and his friends as "secular," and you want nothing to do with them.

"Sometimes the sight of him just makes me want to scream!" a friend once confided to me. "When I see empty beer cans on the sink and he's on the couch watching trashy TV shows—and laughing at them—I can't help thinking of him as the enemy."

Another friend says, "I get so angry because Rob isn't a Christian that sometimes I won't talk to him for days. I put up this wall: *If you won't see things my way, then I don't want anything to do with you.* It's terrible, and I know I'm wrong, but I can't help it."

But we can help it, my friend.

It begins by looking again and again at the cross until we see our-selves as sinners. As Christians, we may be saved, but we're still sinners, and we always will be until we get to heaven. Those feelings of anger, self-righteousness, discontent, and resentment come whenever we start thinking of ourselves more highly than we ought. When that happens, we project an attitude of superiority: *I have the truth and you don't. I'm special and you're not. You're worldly—I'm holy.* When that occurs, it's rarely the unbeliever who's at fault. It's not your husband's sin making him the enemy, but yours.

So what do you do when feelings of anger and resentment start to well up? As with everything else, you run to God. You take all your feel-ings and you dump them at his feet, ask his forgiveness, accept his cleansing. Then you replace your negative thoughts and feelings with the truth:

- My husband is not my enemy; he is the one God has given me to love.

- Loving him doesn't depend on my feelings at the moment but on the actions I take.

- My husband's spiritual condition doesn't make him less of a person or less deserving of respect and common courtesy.

"An angry [woman] stirs up dissention," as the proverb says, "and a hot-tempered one commits many sins" (Proverbs 29:22).

Of course, you already know that.

I hope you also know that we who are in Christ can go to the Father with all our jumbled feelings and troubling emotions anytime, anyplace. He invites us to cast all our cares upon him, for he cares for us (1 Peter 5:7). He cares about us. When we're overwhelmed and lonely, frustrated, fearful, angry, and misunderstood, when we're tired of shifting gears and feeling jerked around, he is there, offering comfort, encouragement, grace, and forgiveness.

- He keeps a record of every tear we shed (Psalm 56:8).

- He quiets us with his love (Zephaniah 3:17).

- He replaces our mourning with gladness and our thoughts of despair with words of praise (Isaiah 61:3).

- He refreshes us when we're weary (Jeremiah 31:25) and renews us when we're weak (Isaiah 40:31).

- He forgives us (1 John 1:9).

- He gives us hope (Romans 15:13).

And hope…helps us endure.

THINK ON THESE THINGS

- **Think** about all the emotions a woman experiences when she is married to an unbeliever or a once-professing Christian who has walked away from the faith. Which ones are most troubling for you? When they overwhelm you, how do you usually react?

- **Study** what God's Word says concerning troubling emotions. Make a list of specific emotions, then using a concordance or Bible dictionary, look up each word. (Also, many Bibles have helps in the back. Find one that has a topical reference list or a subject index. It might say something like "If you feel afraid, turn to Psalm 55.") To get you started, here are a few:

Fearful: 1 John 4:18

Worried or anxious: Matthew 6:27; Philippians 4:6-7; 1 Peter 5:7

- **Apply** a passage of Scripture to each troubling emotion and heartfelt longing as soon as it crops up. Write these verses down or memorize them, and refer to them often. (My most soul-soothing verse is Ephesians 3:20. That's why it appears several times throughout this book.) Remember: ALL our needs are met in the Lord.

- **Consider** one of my favorite statements I tell myself when my feelings start to overwhelm me: "Right now, my feelings don't match my faith." It's okay to cry, but it's not okay to dwell on your fear or worry or sadness. So sometimes I may crawl up on God's lap and cry, but because I've learned to hide his Word in my heart and depend on it for what is true, my faith remains intact.

- What about you? What are some things you know to be true about your relationship with Jesus that can help make your faith more stable and help you weather your stormy emotions?

- "Resting in the Lord does not depend on external circumstances at all, but on your relationship to God himself. Fussing always ends in sin. We imagine that a little anxiety and worry are an indication of how really wise we are; it is much more an indication of how really wicked we are. Fretting springs from a determination to get our own way."

  —Oswald Chambers, *My Utmost for His Highest*

Four

Saved or Unsaved, He's Still a *Guy*

*M*oses burped.

I don't know that for a fact, but I'm pretty sure that while he lived in Egypt at Pharaoh's house and then led the Israelites through the Red Sea and ate manna for breakfast, lunch, and dinner, he burped. Maybe not a long-drawn-out "Listen to me say the alphabet" type of burp, but he burped nonetheless. He probably scratched too.

I remember when I first had this burping epiphany and started thinking about all the godly men I knew and respected. I kept picturing them polishing off a bottle of Faygo vanilla cream soda, then letting one rip. *"ABCDEFG… "* It's quite disconcerting to think about.

A few years ago I had the "pleasure" of riding home from the airport with a pastor friend of mine and his wife. We were all on the same flight from Nashville to Orlando, and he offered me a ride home so I didn't have to take a cab.

Before that, I'd only seen him in "sanctified" situations: church services, picnics, visits to his office. I always knew he was just a guy who happened to be a pastor, but you know how it is. You know it in your head, but because you don't have a Christian adult male living in your house, you somehow think that particular species doesn't behave the way your man generally does. You think Christian men surely don't click the remote control at 55 mph when their wives are trying to watch a TV program or stare blankly when their wives go into minute detail about the dress they saw at Penney's.

Anyway, I can't put my finger on anything specific this pastor did or didn't do on the way home from the airport, but I do remember feeling disillusioned. Like maybe I expected him to pray before stopping at the tollbooths or something. Or discuss the spiritual climate of the nation. As I recall, he had a headache and was irritated about there not being any hot water in the hotel where they had stayed.

When he dropped me off, I remember thinking how guy-like he was. That's when I started thinking about burping and how most men like to do it. And how Moses and the apostles burped. D. James Kennedy, Chuck Swindoll, James Dobson, my husband—they all burp. Guys burp. With gusto and obvious delight.

My point in all of this is simple: Men are not women. They differ from us physically, emotionally, and psychologically. They process information differently than we do; they communicate differently; they have different basic needs.

Here's the kicker: Once a man becomes a Christian, he doesn't change his distinctly male traits. As they say, "Boys will be boys and men will be men." And that, as Martha Stewart would say, is a good thing.

Unfortunately for most husbands, it often takes their wives a long time—if ever—to realize that. Too often women blame their difficulty in communicating and relating with an unbelieving husband on their unequal yoke. *If he were a Christian, he wouldn't feel the need to take off in his truck and drive around for hours by himself.*

But that's not the case.

After reading a few eye-opening books on the subject of gender differences and conducting my own casual research, I discovered many of the conflicts in marriages aren't necessarily caused by spiritual differences. Rather, they're caused by simple gender differences. And if you're unaware of those differences, you may inadvertently cause, or at least aggravate, your spiritual differences.

So in hopes that you can avoid making some major mistakes (or halt the ones you're making now), here's a mini–crash course in Masculinity 101.

Guys Are Primarily Task and Goal Oriented

Way back in the book of Genesis, right after God created man, he put him in the Garden of Eden to work it and care for it, to fill the earth and subdue it. Man was made to work. That's his primary function on the earth, next to loving God.

A man defines himself by what he does, not by his relationships. When introduced, a man will say, "I'm John—I'm in retail sprockets and gears for Yada Yada Industries." When it's his wife's turn, she'll say, "I'm Judy, John's wife, and we have three kids: John Jr., Judy Jr., and JJ."

Men are performance minded. They need to accomplish something, produce something in order to be fulfilled. As a heating mechanic, Barry's not happy unless he can find the problem (no heat) and fix it. When we go for a drive somewhere, he wants to *get there*—and make "good time" doing it.

I, on the other hand, just like the ride and being with him. I rarely care where we're going and don't give a hoot about making good time. What does that mean anyway? It must be a guy thing.

Guys like sports. That's because there's a goal involved: make baskets, get on base, score a touchdown. Most guys don't like figure skating. "What's the point?" a guy asks. "You spin around to music."

When guys get together, it's usually to *do* something: fish, golf, pull an engine out of a car, conduct a meeting. Guys don't "do lunch" or go shopping with other guys. There's no point, no goal. How do you win?

Guys need a goal and a reason to succeed in order to be fulfilled. It's particularly devastating when a man loses his job or even retires. Without meaningful work, a man doesn't have an identity. That's the downside to their task-oriented nature. But there's another, more conflicting, aspect: Men have a hard time with the gospel, that another man (Christ) acquired salvation for us. He did it all, leaving no room for your husband to do it for himself. Men don't like that. It goes against their basic nature.

My pastor tells of a man who came to see him one day. All flustered and fuming the man demanded, "Why can't salvation be done the old-fashioned way—when a man earned it!"

A wise woman will understand this tendency in her husband, encourage him in his God-given instinct to work and produce, and will be patient with her husband's attempts at self-salvation. The Lord knows the inner workings of a man, and he knows how best to reach him.

Guys Are Competitive

It's Super Bowl Sunday. Your husband invites the guys over to watch the game. Before the ball is even snapped, the game in the living room has already begun. They're comparing cars, salaries, who could hold the most liquor in college. They're sizing each other up thinking, "Yeah, I could take him, no problem."

Once the football game starts, they're right there on the field with their favorite team. They're in each other's faces. Then when the game's over, the fans of the winning team are yelling, "We won! We won!" As if by sitting on the couch and eating potato chips, *they* won the game. But don't try to tell them that!

Guys compete—for power, position, women, everything. I have a friend whose husband and father-in-law pull each other's arm hair in an attempt to get the other one to cry or at least wince in pain. My own husband and my daughter's boyfriend do this macho swagger around each other. Barry will flex his muscles and tell me, "I still have the body of a nineteen-year-old."

It's a guy thing.

In his book *What Men Want*, H. Norman Wright asked more than two hundred men, "What is it that you think women do not really understand about men?" One of the answers was, "Our competitiveness is needed to succeed for our families." It's the way God wired men. I'm grateful that Barry possesses this drive to be the strongest and the best. That's what makes him strive for excellence at his job. His competitiveness is a plus when it comes to his being a provider and a protector.

On the other hand, a man's competitive nature often leads to insecurity and jealousy. It's not uncommon for an unbelieving husband to be jealous of his wife's church and the time she spends there, jealous of other Christians—especially other Christian men—and to be jealous of God.

One woman confided that her husband is forever accusing her of cheating on him with men from her church. "He flies into terrible rages and says some awful things to me at times. I can't even repeat what he says. One time he even set a trap for me by leaving a note on my car while I was in church. It supposedly was from a man at church, asking to meet me for coffee." She said she knew immediately it was from her husband, although he denied it. "What would make him do such a thing?" she asked.

Jealousy arouses a husband's fury, says Proverbs 6:34. "Who can stand before jealousy?" (Proverbs 27:4). The competitiveness of a man makes him protective of his wife's affections, and when he feels threatened, he lashes out. However, when it's God who threatens him, he doesn't know how to compete. He can't compete.

A wise woman will make an effort to appreciate her husband's competitive instincts and will take his reasonable display of jealousy as a sign that he's afraid of losing her. The best thing she can do is to assure him by her actions that loving God with her whole heart means having even greater love for him.

Guys Need to Be Needed

"Men are motivated and empowered when they feel needed," writes John Gray in *Men Are from Mars, Women Are from Venus.* "When a man does not feel needed in a relationship, he gradually becomes passive and less energized." He stops trying. He stops caring. He tunes out. As Gray says, not to be needed is a slow death for a man.

If you hadn't noticed, guys love to give advice. It never fails—I'll have something on my mind, such as being overwhelmed by deadlines at work. I may already know what I'm going to do about it, but because I'm a woman and women need to talk things out to relieve stress, I'll sit Barry down and say, "I have to talk. I need to tell you what's bothering me, *even though I already know what I'm going to do.* I'm not asking for advice. I just need to tell you, okay?"

He'll say okay, then as soon as I'm three sentences into my tale of woe, he's got a pad and pencil out, making a list or drawing a diagram of what I should do! He's a guy. Guys love to give advice. They need to be needed.

They need to be needed by their wives.

Because I know that, I never hesitate to ask Barry for his help. Not because I'm lazy or I'm using him, but because I know he needs to be needed. Whenever I get too independent ("I can do this all by myself!"), that's when I feel him slipping away. When a man doesn't feel needed by his wife, that's when he's most tempted to find someone else who does need him.

This poses a conflict to the woman who, all of a sudden, starts taking all her needs to the Lord. *After all, isn't that what I'm supposed to do?*

Of course it is. But an unbelieving husband doesn't understand. He only understands that someone has taken his place. "If she has Jesus, then she must not need me." So he shuts down. He retreats to the couch and watches wrestling on TV. He loses interest in family activities. He stops talking. He loses interest in sex.

A wise woman will understand her husband's need to be needed: as a provider, a protector, a lover, a father to their children, a companion. She will continue to take all her needs to the Lord, but she will also realize that God can and will meet many of her needs through her own husband.

Guys Are Cave Dwellers When Problems Strike

Gray also writes about men's retreating into their "caves" when stressed. Sometimes that means physically retreating (to a garage, den, in front of a computer, fishing, etc.), but many times when a man is working through a problem, his body may be in the same room with his family while his mind is elsewhere. He's unresponsive, preoccupied, distant. Gray calls this withdrawal into a man's own thoughts "going into the cave." The more troublesome the problem, the deeper he goes and the longer he stays.

Gray adds, if he can't resolve his problem, he remains stuck. To get unstuck, he's drawn to solving little, manageable problems: He reads the newspaper, cleans his tools in the garage, plays a video game. "Any challenging activity that initially requires only (a small part) of his mind can assist him in forgetting his problems and becoming unstuck." Then when he returns to his problem, he can more easily redirect his focus.

Trust me when I say my understanding this silly-sounding analogy transformed our marriage.

For Barry, his "cave" is his truck. When he needs to sort things out, he heads for the highway—alone. As a woman who needs to talk things out, this makes no sense to me. *If I could just draw him out, make him talk, I know he would feel better.* But Barry doesn't want to talk things out, he wants to retreat into his cave and mull them over. It's what guys do. However, before I understood this, I'd beg and plead with Barry either to take me with him "so we can talk" or nag him to stay home. He usually ended up frustrated and angry; I ended up frustrated and hurt. Sometimes he'd give in and let me tag along, but it rarely turned out to be the intimate talkfest I'd hoped for. We'd ride around making shallow, if any, conversation until we arrived back home—then Barry would go out again alone, as he had needed to do all along.

Once I learned about this need in men, I quit clinging to Barry's truck bumper and stopped nagging him. I just let him go. Amazingly, when he feels the freedom to deal with stress as a man needs to do, he doesn't stay away nearly as long as he used to.

A wise woman will learn to identify her husband's particular "cave" and respect his need to retreat, especially during times of spiritual conflict. When he's in his cave, when he's feeling the contrast between the two of them, when he's feeling the conviction of sin by the Holy Spirit, while he's in there, a wise woman will make use of the time...and pray.

Guys Fear Losing Control

"Unfamiliar territory makes men nervous," writes Michael Fanstone in *Unbelieving Husbands and the Wives Who Love Them.* He adds that men are easily embarrassed, especially when it comes to going to church. They fear being called on to speak, asked to stand up. They fear not knowing the right things to do, not knowing their way around a Bible, wearing the wrong clothes, not knowing the words to the songs.

Fanstone says it's not uncommon for unbelieving husbands to generously volunteer their time to do things *for* the church instead of going *to* church. "It's more safe and predictable because *they* set the parameters and remain in some degree of control."

Ellen confides, "My husband will play softball on the church team, offer to change a church member's water heater, even have breakfast with the pastor. He does only what he's sure of."

That's because men fear losing control, and the thought of completely abandoning themselves to a God they cannot see is terrifying to a man. A wise woman understands this about her husband and gives him the freedom to test the waters at his own pace and in his own way. For a man who fears losing control, one of the best things his wife can do is simply to be the "aroma of Christ" and a "fragrance of life" (2 Corinthians 2:15-16). To be peculiar but not weird, considerate of his doubts, gentle with his feelings, and patient with his fears.

Guys Fear Being Thought Inadequate

The quickest way to shut a man down is to let him think he's not measuring up. A man constantly measures himself next to the "other guy"— at work, in the neighborhood, at the gym. Brothers measure themselves against each other, against their father. They're always asking, "How am I doing?"

Just as a woman needs to know she's cherished, a man needs to know he's okay—as a father, a provider, a husband, a lover, a man. "A man's deepest fear is that he is not good enough or that he's incompetent," writes John Gray. He gives the age-old example of men not wanting to ask for directions when they're lost, and he cautions women against offering a man advice unless he asks.

"Generally speaking, when a woman offers unsolicited advice or tries to 'help' a man, she has no idea of how critical and unloving she may sound to him," he says. To a man, offering advice is the same as saying, "I don't trust your judgment or your capabilities; I think you're incompetent." He adds, to honor a man by not offering advice is a gift equivalent to his buying a woman a beautiful bouquet of flowers or writing a love note.

At his core, a man yearns to be self-sufficient, adequate, a hero to his family, strong in the eyes of other men, strong in his own eyes. He deeply fears being embarrassed or humiliated. However, this conflicts with the gospel, which calls us to embrace our *in*adequacy, to realize we're not sufficient, not strong. Being "not good enough" is central to Christianity. Men, however, struggle with this, even those who are Christians.

Fortunately, God has the power to change any man's heart. After all, he created men with this trait, that they might receive their sense of adequacy from him. A wise woman will remember that changing hearts is God's job, not hers. When it comes to her husband's spiritual condition, a wise woman will realize even her most loving attempts at "helping" him—offering scriptural answers to his problems, giving him biblical advice at every opportunity—most often isn't what he needs from her. What he needs is loving acceptance.

The apostle Peter, a married man himself, tells the wife of an unbelieving husband what else is needed. He admonishes her to win her unbelieving husband over, not with words, but instead by her behavior and the purity and reverence of her life (1 Peter 3:1-2). And trust God to do the rest.

Guys Fear Being Hypocrites

We've all heard it: The church is filled with hypocrites. It's a standard phrase uttered by unbelieving husbands and is usually near the top of their list of reasons they won't go to church. As my friend Mary Ann told me recently, before her husband came to faith in Christ, he used to sneer, "I'm not going to be one of those hypocrites." That would make her furious! She said she was sure he used the "hypocrite" excuse to spite her, that somehow he was calling her a hypocrite.

But now that he's a committed believer, she's had an opportunity to ask him about it. It seems his words went beyond rhetoric. For Mary Ann's husband, he didn't want to "do church" and only be a halfhearted Christian. He knew he needed it to be total or not at all. The thought of doing less than 100 percent repulsed him. It's not that he didn't want to be around "hypocrites"—he didn't want to be one himself.

Guys fear being hypocrites—in the eyes of others as well as in their own eyes. If they change, they want it to be "for keeps."

Guys Dread Midlife

Although women tend to view their forties as a time of new beginning, men in their late thirties and forties look at this time as their lives being over. This is the time when they dwell on their regrets. *I married too young, wasn't the father I wanted to be. I worked too hard and have nothing to show for it. I wanted to be somebody, but I'm a nobody. All I have to show for my life is a stack of credit card debts. I'm afraid of being impotent. I'm a failure. My family deserves better.*

It's difficult enough for a Christian man to muddle through this time, but a man who doesn't yet know his true worth in God's eyes has no place to turn for solace.

Send a Message to Your Man

Here are some suggestions to help your husband feel appreciated as the man in your life:

- Go to his softball games and pay attention.
- Tell him often that what he does at work is important to you.
- Never belittle or trivialize his work.
- Ask questions about his job. Learn what he does.
- Determine what your husband does well and provide opportunities for him to perform and succeed. Ask him if he would: glue a chair leg, move furniture, change a doorknob, plan a trip, etc.
- Say thank you often.
- Watch your interactions with other men and avoid situations that could be misinterpreted.
- Ask his advice and then take it. If you're not willing to do that, it's better not to ask in the first place.
- Ask for his help.
- Build him up in front of your kids.
- *Never* correct him in public.
- Dream with him, even if you think his dreams are far-fetched. That's what makes them dreams.
- Touch him often, especially when you're listening to him talk.
- Be loyal.
- Enjoy sex.
- Pray and ask God for creative ways to affirm your husband's unique maleness. Then go and do it.

Friend, if your husband is going through a time of midlife darkness, know that even in this, even when it looks bleakest, God is still able to give you everything you need to get through this trial and to equip you to be a minister of his grace to your spouse.

This is the time to know the best thing—perhaps the only thing— you can do is crawl up on the Father's lap and let him hold you as you cry tears of confusion and helplessness for your beloved.

Stay close to the Lord, read up on the subject, get counseling for yourself, and pray like crazy for that man of yours as you give him time and space to work things through.

By now you know that a wise woman knows that it's God and God alone who does it all. He's the one who draws her husband to himself, in his time, in his way, utterly and completely. And as she allows her husband to discover the claims of Christ for himself, when the time comes that he senses the irresistible grace of God beckoning him, it won't be just lip service, but a genuine heart change.

It's the way men are.

It's the way God works.

THINK ON THESE THINGS

- **Think** about the masculine traits that distinguish men from women. What purpose do you think God had when he gave these traits to men? Which traits do you find appealing in your husband? (And you can't say "None.")

- **Study** the story of Abigail and her husband, Nabal, in 1 Samuel 25. What were her actions (and possibly her attitude) toward her husband? Toward David? Study also the story of Esther, a queen married to a pagan king. What were her actions (and attitude) toward her husband?

- **Apply** the example of the woman of noble character in Proverbs 31:10-31 to modern-day marriage. What does the passage say about a woman's role in the family? How is her role different from her husband's?

- **Consider** what H. Norman Wright, author of *The Secrets of a Lasting Marriage,* says about differences between spouses: "We are all different. We're mixtures of various tendencies and preferences. And these are neither right nor wrong." Pray and ask God to show you creative ways to encourage your husband in his maleness and to help you appreciate both of your distinct roles in marriage.

- "Most women know about men's egos, but they see [them] as character flaws. They fail to see that our egos can also be interpreted as positive qualities. Our egos compel us to lead, to serve and to protect women. We need to be valued and respected as family leaders and protectors."

—No name given,

from *What Men Want,* by H. Norman Wright

Being Perfect vs. Being Real

I had sinned grievously. Only three days after answering the Father's call and turning my heart over to Jesus, after only three days of a blissful sin-free existence (or so I thought), I blew it.

Something had happened in the kitchen. If I recall correctly, the upstairs toilet had overflowed for the eightieth time in that many days, and the water had finally seeped through the ceiling and filled the overhead ceiling light in the kitchen with water. Dinner burned on the stove. My then-toddler, Alison, otherwise known as the Amazing Velcro Baby, had adhered herself to my leg and wouldn't let go.

I don't remember the exact details, only that after three days of blathering nonstop to Barry about having been redeemed from sin, washed clean by Christ's blood, set free and forgiven and all the other terms I'd picked up from watching religious television programs, at the exact moment Barry entered the kitchen I swore out loud in front of God and Barry and all the angels in heaven.

Alison, in true toddler fashion, started chanting what she had heard.

While it horrified me, my outburst amused Barry to no end. That's when he uttered—for the first time but not the last—"I thought you were a Christian."

I thought I was too.

Mortified and humiliated, I hung my head in shame. I thought, for certain, I had destroyed my Christian testimony. I didn't know what that meant exactly (again, more tidbits I'd picked up from three days' worth of TV), only that it was vital to "maintain a Christian witness."

In the days following my coming to Christ, the Christians I had worked with in the air force and who had shared their faith with me bombarded me with advice concerning my new life in Jesus. Since they only had a few weeks until my enlistment ended and Barry and I moved away, they gave me a crash course in the "Dos and Don'ts of Being a Christian."

They were sincere and I didn't know any better, so I soaked up everything they said:

- Read the Bible all the way through—and don't skip Numbers, even though it's boring.

- Follow the Ten Commandments. Live the Beatitudes.

- Have a daily quiet time.

- Go to church every time the doors are open: Sunday morning, Sunday evening, and Wednesday nights, too.

- Find a ministry at church and sign up. Be faithful.

- Memorize Scripture.

- Don't smoke. Don't drink. Don't dance. Don't play cards.

- Learn to make Five-Can Casserole and Cherry Dump Cake to bring to potluck dinners.

- Pray without ceasing.

- Witness to everyone you meet.

- Watch what you say and do because people will always be watching you.

I remember jotting down notes as they imparted their wisdom. I so wanted to be a perfect Christian wife, because I knew that was the only way I could "win" Barry to the Lord. Win or work at it, from the advice I garnered from my fellow Christians, I knew it was up to me. It was my responsibility, my duty to make sure Barry could see Christ in me, to see how radically I had changed, how holy I had become.

I vowed to "study to show [myself] approved unto God, a workman that needeth not to be ashamed, rightly dividing the word of truth" (2 Timothy 2:15, KJV). I didn't know what that meant, other than it was written in my notes as something I needed to do. That, and "shun profane and vain babblings" (verse 16).

I knew that meant not swearing.

A Virtuous Woman...Doesn't Live at My House

I had destroyed my Christian witness and vowed it would never happen again. I tried my hardest to do everything written in my notes and to show Barry what being a Christian looked like. I hadn't smoked before, so that wasn't a problem, and I had given up drinking even before coming to Christ. I stunk at playing cards, and nobody ever asked me to play anyway, so even that wasn't a problem (although I never could see why card games were considered "sinful" by some).

However, it was all that other stuff I tried to do and not do that took its toll on me: struggling to maintain a "daily quiet time" so that Barry could see, praying so he could hear. Learning and trying to obey all the "Thou shalt nots" I'd heard from well-meaning friends. As a new believer, I couldn't tell which were from the Bible and which weren't, so I just tried to follow them all.

I have to admit, it used to tear me up inside to be away from Barry all Sunday morning, only to have to leave him again a few hours later to return to church on Sunday night. Every week I'd have an inner tug of war going on: *Go-stay. Go-stay.* I thought if I didn't go, it would hurt my witness and would look as if I wasn't putting God first and would possibly cause Barry to say, "I thought you were a Christian!"

My goal became to be the best Christian example I could be. After all "we are therefore Christ's ambassadors, as though God were making his appeal through us" (2 Corinthians 5:20). I'd also heard it said I might be the only Bible my husband would ever read.

What an awesome challenge. What a tremendous burden.

I surrounded myself with older Christian women and watched them carefully and tried to emulate their actions. I picked up the jargon, developed a sense of what was "worldly" or "carnal" versus what was "spiritual."

To my observation, any music that did not contain the name of Jesus, any TV or radio program that was not broadcast from a Christian station, any activity that didn't include a devotional reading or benediction was considered "worldly" and should be avoided. No being with "worldly" people, no engaging in "worldly" pleasures. More than anything, I didn't want anyone, especially church people, to consider me worldly. Of course, I didn't want God to consider me worldly either, and I wanted Barry to see what a sanctified, set apart, Christian life looked like.

So I set myself apart and worked on being holy. I bit my tongue rather than voice a dissenting opinion during a discussion, and I kept a smile on my face. I studied all the how-tos of godly womanhood and made checklists:

- Rise early and fix him breakfast. *Check.*

- Have his dinner hot and on the table whenever he wants it. *Check.*

- Don't complain if he tracks mud on your freshly washed floors. *Check.*

- Greet him at the door wearing nothing but a smile. *No comment.*

I tried not to show anger. I tried not to complain. I tried to never say a negative word.

I tried to be nice, cheerful, thrifty, loyal, and loving, thinking that's what it meant to be a Christian. To emulate Christ and follow the rules. To lose all sense of self, to try and be and do the ideal.

For all my efforts, all I reaped was a sense of having failed miserably. Whenever I didn't exhibit any of the Christlike qualities I tried so hard to achieve, I was fair game for Barry to point it out. Sometimes he did; sometimes he didn't. Either way, I didn't want to give him that opportunity. I felt I owed it to God to be my husband's Bible. He was "reading" me anyway, and I didn't want to let God down. His reputation was at stake. If I failed, it reflected on the Lord's power to change a human life.

Except...by trying to present a sanctified, spiritual life to my husband, all he saw was an impossible set of standards that didn't bring me life or joy, only an uncomfortableness in my own body. I squirmed a lot. Twisted inside. All I wanted was to escape this pressure of having to live up to an ideal for my husband's sake and at the same time stay uncontaminated by his "worldly" influences.

On more than one occasion he'd look at me sitting on the other side of the room from him, my nose in the Bible or a Christian book, trying to be godly, trying to stay away from the ball game or movie on TV, and he'd just shake his head in disgust. Then I'd shake mine and call him a pagan or a heathen under my breath.

How arrogant of me! How self-righteous.

To my way of thinking, he could come to church or a church event with me if he chose, he could sit down with me and watch Christian TV or listen to my music, he could come over to my side, the holy side, but I wasn't about to join him in any activity that might taint me. Jesus may have hung out with sinners and prostitutes, but I wasn't going to.

Somewhere along the way, my attitude had shifted. It didn't take long either. No longer did I want him to experience knowing Christ because it would give him an eternal hope and sense of wholeness and joy down to his core. I had forgotten that I was (and am) still a sinner. Instead, I took on an attitude of having been called by God because of some inherent spark of goodness within me. To have my husband see this goodness and therefore be convinced that he wanted it for himself became my motivation. *He must see Christ in me!* That way I could "win" him to the Lord, and everyone would know what a godly woman I am, maybe even rise up and call me blessed.

My husband eventually did rise up, but not to call me blessed. It was on my birthday in 1978. He had had enough and that morning told me, "It's a good thing we don't have any money, because I'd divorce you today and send you back to your parents."

He left for work and I was left stunned. My immediate thought was one of self-protection and self-justification. It wasn't my fault—it was God's fault. Even Jesus said he didn't come to bring peace to a family, but a sword that often causes division and un-peace (Matthew 10:34).

But it wasn't God's fault. Yes, the gospel and the Spirit of God create a separation between a believer and an unbeliever, but in my marriage the main problem was me. In my attempt to be a perfect Christian example, I had become a perfect Christian pain in the neck.

As for the rest of the "I'd divorce you today" story, it has an amazing ending that I'm saving for another chapter. So keep reading.

"Oh, You Dear Idiots!"

In talking to and corresponding with women who struggle with this whole idea of being a Christian example to their husbands, it's not uncommon for them to voice their confusion, frustration, and mixed emotions. One woman told me, "I think having to always maintain a perfect Christian example at home is why I'm often depressed. My home life is so stressful because I want to win him to Christ through *my* behavior and exemplary love. I've had so many well-meaning church members tell me to be patient and he will come to God because he sees me being so loving toward him when he treats me like trash. But I confess, sometimes I get so tired of trying. I have no energy and no love, yet I must be perfect because he might be watching me. I don't want to be a stumbling block to him!"

Another woman said, "I'm always thinking I have to maintain a 'perfect witness' or Christian example. This comes up at church—not overtly, but small comments (people make) cause me to feel that if I were a good Christian, my husband would see it clearly and join in."

She added, "It's also a weapon my husband uses against me when we argue: 'If you're such a great Christian and God loves you so much, then why did you _____.' Fill in the blank with anything from 'marry me' to 'tell a fib yesterday.'"

If this describes your life, if you feel pressured by the need to be perfect, whether the pressure comes from your husband, well-meaning friends, or your own sense of what a Christian should be, then I have good news for you: In the book of Galatians, the apostle Paul calls you a "dear idiot." Then he tells you why and how not to be one anymore.

Our struggle isn't with our husbands as much as it is with ourselves. We initially came to Christ because we knew we were bankrupt. "Nothing in my hand I bring, simply to Thy cross I cling," as it says in the hymn "Rock of Ages."

We understood that it's "by grace [we] have been saved, through faith—and this not from [our]selves, it is the gift of God—not by works, so that no one can boast" (Ephesians 2:8-9). And we were so relieved to be free from the penalty and the power of sin, so grateful to be counted among God's own dearly loved children.

But then somewhere along the way, Christ's death became not enough. Oh, we would never say that or even think it, but we began to live it. *His death was enough to pay my ticket to heaven, but now I've got to pay my own way through life.* Maybe we think we need to repay our debt. Maybe we think God will be mad if we don't work hard to clean up our own acts. After all, we tell our kids, "You made the mess, now you clean it up!"

Besides, we like being good and having others see and admire us. We take pleasure in our good deeds and compare them with the deeds of others. *Next to you, I'm not so bad. Next to her, I'm even better. Next to my husband—the lump over there on the couch, with a beer in one hand and the remote in the other—I'm pretty darn good.*

We certainly don't say *that* out loud…but we think it. And the lump on the couch hears it from all the way across the room and thinks to himself, "If that's what a Christian is like, then no thank you."

Be honest. Do you blame him?

Here's what the apostle Paul had to say:

> You crazy Galatians! *[You dear idiots.]* Did someone put a hex on you? Have you taken leave of your senses? Something crazy has happened, for it's obvious that you no longer have the crucified Jesus in clear focus in your lives. His sacrifice on the Cross was certainly set before you clearly enough.
>
> Let me put this question to you: How did your new life begin? Was it by working your heads off to please God? Or was it by responding to God's Message to you? Are you going to continue this craziness? For only crazy people would think they could complete by their own efforts what was begun by God....
>
> Answer this question: Does the God who lavishly provides you with his own presence, his Holy Spirit, working things in your lives you could never do for yourselves, does he do these things because of your strenuous moral striving *or* because you trust him to do them in you? (Galatians 3:1-5, MSG)

In other words, in the battle between being perfect and being real, the answer lies in our understanding of the gospel. The Galatians began the same way you and I began: Christ alone—his perfect life and perfect death for my imperfection. Period. Then early Christians allowed themselves to be swayed in their thinking—Christ plus circumcision. Now, that's not a temptation for us; today circumcision is a medical procedure performed on our sons. For us "circumcision" is anything we think earns us favor with God: our spiritual disciplines, church membership and attendance, trying hard, being as perfect as we can be.

To that, Paul said, "The obvious impossibility of carrying out such a moral program should make it plain that no one can sustain a relationship with God that way. The person who lives in right relationship with God does it by embracing what God arranges for him. *Doing things for God is the opposite of entering into what God does for you*" (Galatians 3:11, MSG, emphasis mine).

As soon as my Christian actions become my focus, "maintaining my witness," I negate Christ's death. As a result, what I present to my husband isn't the real gospel; it's just a religion—what I do for God. In my attempt to model Christ, I don't. He then gets a false picture, and I'm missing out on experiencing the grace and freedom I have in Christ—and we're both miserable.

A Virtuous Woman Lives at My House After All

The question is, how do I go from feeling I have to be perfect to simply being real? Recently, I posed that question to my pastor-friend Ron. He said to go from "perfect" to real a person needs a bridge: the knowledge of the love of God for his children. Then he reminded me of a prayer Paul made on behalf of the church at Ephesus:

> I pray that out of [God the Father's] glorious riches he
> may strengthen you with power through his Spirit in your
> inner being, so that Christ may dwell in your hearts
> through faith. And I pray that you, being rooted and
> established in love, may have power, together with all the
> saints, to grasp how wide and long and high and deep is
> the love of Christ, and to know this love that surpasses
> knowledge—that you may be filled to the measure of all
> the fullness of God. (Ephesians 3:16-19)

Go back and read that again, slowly. Ask the Holy Spirit to help you understand it, to experience it, to own it.

Now think about what it's like to be around someone whom you know loves you dearly. You're comfortable, free. You can be yourself with this person, faults and all. That's how God wants us to be in his presence. To be so filled with the knowledge of his love and acceptance that we're secure enough to simply be ourselves: works in progress, sinners saved by grace.

Yeah, but my husband thinks Christians are supposed to be perfect, and he's not going to understand about grace.

I knew you would say that, so I asked Ron for some practical advice. He told me to remind you that you're going to blow it, and the best thing—the real thing—you can do as you live out your Christianity before your husband is to let him see it. Let him see (he sees it anyway), and let him know you're sorry.

Show him what repentance looks like. When you lose your temper or lie to someone on the phone, either before or after he points it out, tell him, "I shouldn't have done that. I was wrong."

Let him see you struggle—with your overeating, your overspending, your inconsistencies and weaknesses. (He sees them anyway.) Let him know it's difficult, but that God isn't through changing you. That being a Christian is a work in progress. Two steps forward, one step back—sometimes even three steps back. But that God loves you anyway, because you're his.

A virtuous woman knows that any virtue she has is not hers to begin with. Any goodness she shows is Christ's alone.

A virtuous woman lives honestly. She knows she's been set apart by God only because of his mercy and not because of her merit.

Like Paul, she wrestles with doing the things she knows she shouldn't and not doing the things she knows she should.

Like King David, she admits her sin and basks in God's forgiveness.

She's not perfect. She doesn't pretend to be.

She keeps returning to the "bridge" and to the Cross and continually asks God to fill her with the knowledge of his love until she feels secure enough to be real. When she's real, she's free—and it's for freedom that Christ has set us free (Galatians 5:1).

And that, my friend, is the Bible we want our husbands to read.

THINK ON THESE THINGS

- **Think** about how easily Christians fall into the "maintaining a good witness" trap. In what ways have you felt you couldn't be real with non-Christians? What message does this send?

- **Study** what the Bible says about "light." Jesus talked about believers being light in our world in Matthew 5:14-16. Using a concordance, discover what it means to be a light in the darkness. Where does our light come from? Can it ever go out?

- **Apply** the concept of being a light to an unbelieving husband by first reading 2 Corinthians 4. Verse 7 talks about "jars of clay." How is being real—a jar of clay—a more effective means of living out the gospel than pretending we're something we're not?

- **Consider** the concept of being perhaps the only Bible your husband will ever read. If that's the case, what is he reading? How does it line up with the truth of Scripture? (Don't despair if you start thinking you've blown it. That's the whole point—we're always going to blow it, but we can keep returning to the Cross for forgiveness and grace. *That's* the Bible our husbands need to "read" in us.)

- "Too many women were raised to be *people-pleasers:* Please the men. Please the grown-ups. Please your friends. Please everybody! True liberation is when women come to faith in Jesus Christ, develop inner security and become God-pleasers—strong enough to break out of the mold, accept God's assignments and make a radical difference in their world."

—Bill Hybels, *Honest to God?*

Six

Love Does *What?!*

*B*arry and I fell in love with each other in the Tampa airport. That in itself is not newsworthy. That we had already been married twelve or so years *is*.

We may have loved each other before then, but that was the moment we knew it. We were traveling back to California, where we lived at the time, after a difficult visit with Barry's parents.

I always felt that Barry's mother didn't like me. She thought I was odd. She couldn't understand my Christian zeal. Why couldn't I just leave her son alone with all this Jesus stuff? Mind my own business. Be normal.

Barry felt torn: Make peace with me for the sake of his sanity and our two daughters, or make peace with his mother. That particular visit with her was exceptionally hard because she was sick (although no one knew it), which affected her emotions.

She and I got into it.

Twelve or so years' worth of her pent-up emotions spilled out. But that's not important. She's gone now. What is important: After all our years together, after marrying in haste, after being emotionally and spiritually miles apart for most of that time, Barry chose me over his parents, something I'd never known him to do before.

One night he exploded. "This is my wife," he said, "and you can't treat her this way."

He wanted to take the girls and me and leave just then, but I pleaded with him not to. Although I wanted nothing more, I knew we couldn't leave. I'm glad we didn't—that was the last time we ever saw my mother-in-law alive.

After a few uncomfortable days, Barry's parents took us to the airport. While we waited for our flight, Barry presented me with a ring: his baby ring, with a tiny diamond and ruby chip.

"In the early days," he said, "I didn't really love you. But now I do."

"I didn't love you either," I confessed, "but I do now too."

It sounds ridiculous, but the day we told each other "I didn't love you" was the day *we* fell in love. However, *I* had fallen in love with Barry long before then. That happened on the day I fell in love with Jesus. I just didn't know it until that day in the airport.

Wherefore Love?

Friend, I realize you may be reading this and thinking, *That's dandy for her. She loves her husband and he loves her. They've found happily ever after. But my life is not like Nancy's. In fact, it's the opposite: I once loved my husband, but now I don't. We're too different. We're more like tolerant roommates. Sometimes not even that.*

You may even be toying with the idea of divorce and finding a Christian man to love. Trust me, you wouldn't be the first to think that. But just stay with me. I prayed before I started writing this that you would find hope.

And love.

I have a message to you from the God who knows your every hurt and heartache:

> I will give you a new heart and put a new spirit in you; I will remove from you your heart of stone and give you a heart of flesh. And I will put my Spirit in you and move you to follow my decrees and be careful to keep my laws. (Ezekiel 36:26-27)

He says:

> Therefore, as God's chosen people, holy and dearly loved, clothe yourselves with compassion, kindness, humility, gentleness and patience. Bear with each other and forgive whatever grievances you may have against one another. (Colossians 3:12-13)

And:

> Over all these virtues put on love, which binds them all together in perfect unity. (Colossians 3:14)

Did you note the sequence? God removes and replaces our hearts of stone with hearts of flesh. Pliable, moldable. Lovable.

He calls us chosen and dearly loved. He takes delight in us and rejoices over us with singing (Zephaniah 3:17).

He loves us. He loves us deeply. As my favorite Bible teacher, Steve Brown, says, "He's quite fond of us." Not because we're hot stuff—don't ever let yourself think that—but because in Christ we're his.

That, then, is the basis for loving others. We love because we are loved. God loves us first, best, completely. *Then* we can love our husbands. We have the capability; we have the resources. We're filled to overflowing.

You may think, *Thank you very much for sharing, Nancy, but I still don't feel loving toward my husband. It's too hard.*

I knew you'd say that. I also know that I can't convince you otherwise. But the Spirit working in you and the Word of God transforming you can. So when you start thinking you can't—by the way, when you say you can't, you're really saying you won't—just remember:

- If God began a good work in you (and he did), he said he would finish what he started (Philippians 1:6).

- He gives you both the desire to love and the ability to do so (Philippians 2:13).

- He created you for some awesome good works (Ephesians 2:10).

- He tells you plainly that you *can* do all things through his strength (Philippians 4:13).

- When you go through tough times, he's right there with you (Isaiah 43:2).

- He holds you in his grip (Psalm 73:23).

Dear friend, don't read any farther until you know you're loved madly, deeply, eternally by God. Unless you know that, all the practical how-tos and advice will only be a to-do list and will bring you despair. So if you need to, set this book down, grab your Bible, and go sit with the One who calls himself your Husband (Isaiah 54:5). When you return, we'll talk about what love looks like in a marriage.

Love Is...an Attitude

Funny thing about God: Once we're his, he often requires us to do what we think is impossible. For many women—and not just those married to unbelievers—respecting their husbands falls into the impossibility category.

"I'd respect him if he wasn't such a jerk," a woman named Christy told me. "He's rude, he's mean. He's drunk every other night, and the rest of the time he's on the couch watching trash on TV. Surely God doesn't expect me to respect that?"

As wives, we're not commanded to respect our husband's actions and choices, but we are commanded to respect *him.* Maybe not what he does, but definitely who he is and the position he holds within the family. He is a person whom God created in his own image, and he is husband to his wife.

In every Bible translation I could find, Ephesians 5:33 tells wives they *must* respect their husband. One version uses the word "honor," several say "reverence," and the *Amplified Bible* says wives are to respect *and* reverence, notice, regard, honor, prefer, venerate, and esteem, defer to, praise, love, and admire exceedingly.

Even if your husband acts like a jerk.

In his book *Each for the Other: Marriage As It's Meant to Be,* Bryan Chapell writes, "Because we most deeply love what we regard most highly, a wife longs to think highly of her husband because intuitively she knows her capacity to love resides in that regard. What the Bible commands only harmonizes with what an unselfish and unwounded heart affirms."

We want to respect the man we've married, but we don't. We're selfish and wounded, so we withhold our respect. *He doesn't deserve it. When he does, then I'll give it.*

But God says he does deserve it, and not based on his actions or personality or whether or not he attends the church picnic. A wife (that's you and me) must (not an option) respect (go back and review that *Amplified* definition if you need to) her husband. It's based on relationship, not on feelings or merit.

"Your husband might irritate you, belittle you, offend you, ignore you, or basically nauseate you, but admiration looks beyond what he does to who he is. It's unconditional," writes Gary Smalley in his book *For Better or for Best.*

In it he tells women that the law of admiration, or respect, is the basis of all lasting, growing relationships. Plus, he says you don't even have to like your husband to admire him. "Admiring someone is a choice, a decision, a commitment, an act of our will. It's telling ourselves, 'God loves and values that person, and so can I.'"

What we think is who we become. In other words, our thoughts determine our attitudes, which determine our actions. If I think my husband is a jerk, I'll treat him like a jerk. But if I think about how he's made in God's image, then I'll treat him differently. Respectfully. Men need to know they're respected.

Chapell says a woman isn't to offer respect just to feed her husband's ego, however. It also benefits her as well. "The more she treasures her husband, the more precious a woman will find their union and the more rewarding their relationship will become to her. The woman who longs for the bonds of love finds her deepest satisfaction is providing the support that secures the relationship for which she longs. Conversely, the woman who does not offer her husband respect denies herself the potential for intimacy."

So I posed this challenge to Christy. I told her, "Okay, pick one thing you admire or respect about your husband—and you can't say 'Nothing.'"

At first she didn't want to answer. She was used to thinking of him only as a "lazy jerk." Finally she told me, "He let me enroll the kids in Christian school, and he'll go to school activities."

That's *big.*

I told her that shows he cares about their kids, and that's a good start. Now she has something to build on. She was skeptical, but at least she was willing to try. *Dis*respect certainly wasn't pleasing anyone, most of all God.

What about you? What about your husband? Take some time and think about what you can respect or admire about him—and you can't say "Nothing." Even if it's only one thing—even if it's only "He remembers to put the twist-tie back on the bread bag"—name something. Every day add to your list.

Then go beyond what he does to who he is.

If it's too hard, ask the Lord to help you. He knows who your husband is.

And he wants you to know too.

Love...Submits

I'll never forget the time I killed my husband. After we got out of the air force, we moved to Portland, Maine, where I found a church, met some friends, settled in. Three years later, as a dutiful, submissive wife, I didn't complain (much) when Barry decided we should move all the way to California. My dad had offered him a job and the opportunity to learn a new trade as a machinist.

So we moved.

I found a church, met some friends, got reacquainted and reattached to my family, and settled in. After a year or so, Barry discovered he didn't like machine shop work, so he found a different job.

Not a problem. Life was swell.

Then I got pregnant with Laura—and two weeks later Barry got laid off.

I killed him several months after that.

As he diligently looked for work day after day, Barry became increasingly aware that he might not be able to find a job where we lived. "We might have to move again," he would tell me.

But I didn't want to. I didn't ever want to leave my parents or brothers or sister again. So I dug in my heels and said, "No!"

I firmly, loudly, obstinately told him, "I won't leave—you can find work here, I just know it." I invoked God's name and told him the Lord would provide for us *right here.*

That's what eventually killed him, although I didn't know it right away. It wasn't until I overheard Barry's end of a phone conversation with his mother. Like a death rattle he gasped, "Mom—I'm *dying.* I can't find work, and Nancy doesn't want to leave her family. I don't know what to do!"

For Barry to say that to his mom, I knew he had to be in pain—and I had caused it. Not only wasn't I pleasing my husband, but also the God I said I loved. Clearly, I was violating his command to submit "as to the Lord" (Ephesians 5:22).

In God's design of marriage there can be only one head of the family—and it's not me. Not the wife. Man was created to lead. Woman was created to follow, to adapt, to arrange herself under.

Chapell writes, "The idea is that as a woman submits to her husband, she looks over his shoulder to see the Lord who is saying, 'You are ultimately doing this not for him but for me.'"

When it's done for the Lord, it's so much easier, my friend Sherry told me. Although her husband is now a committed believer, she still remembers years ago resenting and hating the thought of folding his underwear. She said every time she emptied a pile of laundry out on the bed, her stomach knotted: a symptom of her deep resentment of having to submit to a man she thought didn't deserve it.

Then one day she realized she wasn't doing it for Dennis but was, in fact, doing it for Jesus. "Okay, Lord," she'd say, "I'm folding these for you." After a while her resentment ceased, and she discovered her feelings for her husband had also softened.

As Chapell points out, "Submission is an act of worship whose primary purpose is to honor God." Except in matters clearly prohibited by Scripture, a wife is to submit to her husband *as to the Lord*. In all things. That does not mean going along with sin or participating in evil. Nor does it mean subjecting herself to abuse or allowing herself to be treated as a doormat. (What to do when your husband wants you to do something you know violates God's Word is something I'll discuss in chapter 12.)

Submission also doesn't mean not having an opinion or input. Think of the wife's submissive role as an act of voluntary yielding. A corporate VP, an airline copilot, a sea captain's first mate. Different functions with equal dignity.

In a marriage, true submission involves a wife willingly following her husband's lead while trusting in the Lord's covenant promises to her as his child: to keep her safe from sin and to hold her tight.

As for me, when I realized my refusal to move away from my family was suffocating Barry, I immediately told him how sorry I was, and that I would go with him anywhere he led us.

We ended up moving three hundred miles away, and then seven years later moved again, from California to Florida. With each move I discovered abundant blessings and more than sufficient grace. I learned my lesson: Submission isn't always easy, but it's always ultimately good.

I admit, it's not hard to submit to Barry because he's a good man. But even if he weren't, the Scriptures are clear. Besides, it's not about the goodness of the man but the goodness of the Lord.

So if you're at a place where you think your situation is too difficult, go back to the beginning of this chapter. Get yourself loved by God, find something to admire and respect about your husband, then ask the Holy Spirit to change your thinking about submission.

Then go do it. Do it from a heart of gratitude. Do it for Jesus…and you'll be blessed.

Love…Acts

In *The Message,* Eugene Peterson offers this paraphrase of the well-known "love chapter" of 1 Corinthians:

> Love never gives up.
> Love cares more for others than for self.
> Love doesn't want what it doesn't have.
> Love doesn't strut,
> Doesn't have a swelled head,
> Doesn't force itself on others,
> Isn't always "me first,"
> Doesn't fly off the handle,
> Doesn't keep score of the sins of others,
> Doesn't revel when others grovel,
> Takes pleasure in the flowering of truth,
> Puts up with anything,
> Trusts God always,
> Always looks for the best,
> Never looks back,
> But keeps going to the end. (1 Corinthians 13:4-7)

Love goes beyond feeling to action. In fact, it's possible to love someone you don't particularly like because love is a deliberate act, a willful choice. God chose to love you and me, not because we're just so cute and lovable that he couldn't resist. If his love for us depended on our lovableness, then we'd be fried toast.

No, love sets its will on an object and says, "I choose you." Then love acts. It does stuff, practical stuff, solely for the benefit of the one being loved and without thought of getting anything in return. No strings attached, no price tag. If there were, it wouldn't be love.

A helpful book on the subject of practical expressions of love is *The Five Love Languages* by Gary Chapman. In it he says people express and receive or understand love in different ways. He identifies these five ways or "languages" as: Quality Time, Words of Affirmation, Gifts, Acts of Service, and Physical Touch.

He also says, "If you express love in a way your spouse doesn't understand, he…won't realize you've expressed your love at all!" The key then is to discover your husband's primary love language and then find specific ways to "speak" it.

My primary love language is Words of Affirmation. Tell me I'm doing a good job, tell me what you like about me, and I can feed off it for a week. However, that doesn't work for Barry. Not that he doesn't appreciate a sincere compliment, but his primary love language is Acts of Service.

To Barry, "If I shout love poems from the rooftop, but fail to return the neighbor's Weedwacker after he's asked me to, I'm only making a big noise and he doesn't feel loved" (1 Corinthians 13:1, my paraphrase).

Knowing that acts of service speak love to my husband's heart makes finding practical expressions of love for him so much easier. Not that I exclude any of the other "languages," but I concentrate on what I know he needs most.

Sometimes that means doing things I'd rather not do: sweeping the driveway, checking my own oil in my car, going to the market across town because it has the bread he likes. These are such little things, but I know they speak volumes.

Volumes of love.

Ultimately, it's love that softens a hard heart. It's love that breaks a stubborn will and causes a stiffened knee to bend. It's love—God's love—that draws an unrepentant sinner into his presence. And I'm not talking just about our husbands, but about us as well.

"Dear friends," writes John the apostle, "since God so loved us, we also ought to love one another" (1 John 4:11). Love that's:

from a heart that's first been loved by God

with respect

in submission

through purposeful action

for the glory of God.

———⚬———

THINK ON THESE THINGS

- **Think** about and name some of the common assumptions (even misconceptions) about the admonition for wives to submit to their husbands. What are some reasons God might have for requiring wives to be submissive to their husbands?

- **Study** what the Bible (not anyone's opinion) says about submission. Begin with our perfect example, Jesus, in Philippians 2:1-16. Read also Ephesians 5:21-24, Colossians 3:15-18, James 4:6-8, and 1 Peter 3:1-6. What are some of the ways you can show submission to your husband? (Note: If your husband asks you to do something that violates God's law, then you must refuse him. Your highest allegiance always belongs to the Lord. We submit first to him.)

- **Apply** the principle of biblical submission by thinking of the word "adapt." We are to adapt or "fit in" with our husbands' plans. The Bible calls Sarah our example (1 Peter 3:6). Read about her in Genesis 12 and Genesis 16–21. How did she adapt to her husband's plans? What does that say about her respect for her husband?

- **Consider** how God has called you to fit into your own husband's plans and to show him respect and love through service. What are some practical ways you can do this for him? Is there something God is calling you to do that you've been reluctant to do up until now? Just think: You never know how your acts of true biblical submission will speak to your husband's heart. (But do it for the Lord.) Ask him to make you willing to be the wife he's called you to be.

- "Rational, volitional love.... That is the kind of love to which the sages have always called us. It is intentional. That is good news to the married couple who have lost all of their "in love" feelings. If love is a choice, then they have the capacity to love.... Love is the attitude that says, 'I am married to you, and I choose to look out for your interests.' Then the one who chooses to love will find appropriate ways to express that decision."

  —Gary Chapman, *The Five Love Languages*

Home Building 101

*I*n my marriage, I am the Designated Flashlight Holder. If Barry goes up into the attic or under the car, as the DFH, it's my job to hold the flashlight.

I do other things too, like hand him tools, run back and forth from garage to kitchen for ice water or Gatorade, dash to the auto parts store for gaskets or whatever. Sometimes I get to keep the ladder steady. Other times, like when he's checking the fuse box, I get to shout "Now!" when he throws the switch that turns the power on or off in a particular room.

But mostly, I hold the flashlight.

It's an important job. After all, Barry can't do what needs doing unless he can see.

The problem comes when I want to do more. Or I want to do things my way. Or I think I know best, that I'm a better spouse or parent because I'm a Christian. When I start thinking that holding a flashlight—being a helper and an encouragement to my husband—isn't enough, then I invite all kinds of misery upon myself as well as my entire household.

If I ever doubt that, all I have to do is look at the patched ceiling out in the garage. I won't go into details; just know that if you're ever up in the attic holding the flashlight as your husband runs an electrical line, and he tells you, "Stay on the rafters," do it.

If you don't, if you step off the rafters thinking that you can be of greater help by standing on the Sheetrock and telling him your better way to do what he's doing, you *will* create a skylight where you might not want one. Plus, your leg *will* dangle from the hole that you made—and your husband *will not* be amused. Not only that, you will have destroyed your house by your own foolish actions. And I'm not talking about just the hole in the ceiling.

In *The Living Bible,* Proverbs 14:1 says, "A wise woman builds her house, while a foolish woman tears hers down by her own efforts." As we take a deeper look at "house building," especially as it pertains to a spiritually mismatched marriage, we're going to start with the end of the proverb and how we as wives tear our houses down by our own efforts, then we'll discuss how we can build or rebuild them.

Demolition Queens and Home Wreckers

I missed my calling in life. I could make big bucks going into demolition work. Once I poured an entire pot of hot red wax down the kitchen sink and turned on the cold water. (This was after I'd started a fire on the stove and dusted the kitchen with cornstarch and baking soda trying to put the fire out.) It resulted in the washing machine and dishwasher backing up and flooding the laundry room and kitchen, not to mention completely plugging the entire kitchen drainpipes. By the time the plumber got done, we had the world's most expensive red candle.

As I said, I'm good at demolition work. It's easy. It comes naturally.

Fortunately, when all that's at stake is a hole in the ceiling or clogged pipes, it's fairly easy to fix. Worst-case scenario: Even if I accidentally burned my house down to the ground, it could be rebuilt with concrete and wood.

A marriage, however, is a different story altogether.

Several years ago I wrote an article for the local newspaper about servant evangelism. The concept involves Christians' showing God's love to their community in practical ways—no strings attached. No passing out tracts, no preaching. Just serving.

The pastor leading the project told me of a study another church had conducted. In that study they determined that it takes approximately seven or eight positive encounters with the gospel before a person is open to the idea of becoming a Christian. (Note: This isn't an exact science, only a general theory based on observation.)

Let's take your husband as an example—we'll call him Bob—and apply this theory to a spiritually unequal marriage. Picture a straight-line graph with zero in the middle. Let's put Bob at minus-twelve.

In order for his heart to be open to receiving Christ, he needs to be at plus-eight. So maybe a Christian he works with corners Bob in the break room one day and shoves a gospel tract in his hand and says, "Repent or burn, buddy." Bob's turned off and goes down to minus-thirteen.

Maybe the following week he observes someone returning too much change to a grocery cashier and then sees the person get into a car with a Christian bumper sticker on the back. Bob's touched by the person's honesty, and as he thinks about it, he goes up a notch on the graph.

The tricky part is, with the continual positive and negative gospel encounters going on, no one except God ever really knows exactly where Bob is on his graph. Nevertheless, God has called you as Bob's wife and me as Barry's wife to be positive influences, to be encouragers rather than discouragers, to be house builders, not home wreckers.

When it comes to tearing our houses down, one common tendency is trying to be our husbands' personal Holy Spirit. It goes like this: I know perfectly well that it's the Spirit who convicts a person of sin, opens closed eyes, melts a cold heart. I know all that. But…frankly, he doesn't do it fast enough for me. That's why I think I should help.

Friend, if you're anything like me, this is one of the hardest areas to let go. There's an event, a seminar, a class, a concert, and you just *know* that if only your husband would go, on the way home he'd be blubbering like a baby, asking you to help him give his life to Jesus.

Or there's a guy at church who's such a godly example that you *know* if only he and your husband could get together for a golf game, he would lead your husband to the Lord by the third hole. So you plan and scheme ways to manipulate circumstances, and then when your plans fall through or backfire—the godly man cheats at golf or the conference speaker drones on and on and puts even his own wife to sleep—you're disappointed and ticked. At God, at yourself, at your husband.

There goes a shingle off the roof as I tear my house down by my own efforts.

Another way we play the Holy Spirit is by serving as our husbands' conscience. You plead, "You promised you'd come to church with me 'soon,' and it's been three months since you said it. You don't want to be a liar in front of your children, do you?"

There goes the back porch.

Or you shoot him a disapproving look if he does something you think is "secular" or "worldly."

There goes the front door.

There goes your house, and there goes your husband halfway down the street as he tries to escape.

A man named Rick told me, "With my wife, it's constant. If she's not blasting the religious music, she's got the religious TV programs going. She's always reading to me out of the Bible, trying to get me to listen. I can't take it! If I wanted to believe and go to church before, I don't want to now. When she starts in, I just go out and talk to God myself. I tell God, 'I guess she's got to get this out of her system, but I sure wish she'd hurry it up.'"

In a later conversation, Rick's wife confessed, "I know I can be overbearing at times, but who else is going to lead him to the Lord? I'm the only Christian he knows, and I'm his wife. Besides, if 'Faith comes by hearing and hearing by the Word of God,' then isn't it my job to give him the Word?"

The apostle Peter answered that question in his first letter. He tells wives, "In the same way [as Christ] be submissive to your husbands so that, if any of them do not believe the word, *they may be won over without words by the behavior of their wives, when they see the purity and reverence of your lives*" (1 Peter 3:1-2, emphasis mine).

Solomon adds his wisdom when he cautions, "A nagging wife annoys like constant dripping" (Proverbs 19:13, TLB). Drip long enough or loud enough and chances are your husband will tell you to dry up, or words to that effect.

It all comes down to this: Do we trust God or not? If we believe and trust his Word and rest in the truth that it's *his* Holy Spirit who convicts men of their sin and draws them to the Father, then we will relinquish the need to control our situation. (News flash: We're not in control anyway.)

Paula remembers sitting next to her husband at a church Christmas program and fretting over whether or not the pastor's message would include all the points she thought he needed to cover and whether or not her husband was listening attentively enough. "I sat there with my Bible open, following along with my finger in case Alan should glance over and want to read along," she recalls.

As her stomach knotted because she felt he wasn't "getting it," Paula says she heard the rebuking words of Jesus to Peter who had been fretting over "that other guy." Jesus told him, "*He's* none of your business. *You* follow me" (John 21:22, my paraphrase).

That's when Paula decided, if the Holy Spirit is God (and he is), and if he's all-mighty and all-powerful, then any of our puny attempts to take over his role in our husbands' lives are, at best, ludicrous. At worst, they accomplish the opposite of what we intend and create a pile of rubble out of our houses. How much greater our peace to simply trust that God has already sanctified our spouse—set him apart—because of the covenant of faith he has made with us as believers. We can trust him to draw and convict our husbands.

Another equally destructive tendency is to treat an unbelieving or spiritually distant husband like the enemy. He makes fun of your faith, bad-mouths your Christian friends behind their backs. Says the church is full of hypocrites. Laughs at Christian radio. So…you go on the defensive. You hide in the bedroom listening to Christian CDs when he's watching TV. You take every jab personally. You sound retreat, bury your head, tiptoe around waiting for land mines to blow you to bits.

Or you become offensive. *Very* offensive. You tsk tsk at his behavior, glare at him when he swears. You refuse to let him tuck the kids into bed in case he should say something you don't approve of. You categorize everything into secular vs. spiritual, godly vs. ungodly. You wait for him to do something "ungodly," then pounce on him when he does. "Aha!" you say. "I knew you'd do that!" And you keep your little scorepad up to date.

You: 3,654; Him: −6,298

Either way, defense or offense, you've lost the sense of oneness with your husband—and you blame *him*. After all, he's the enemy. (Another news flash: As long as you're keeping score, Jesus said we're to forgive "seventy times seven" when our husbands offend us. At 490 times per offense, that means you're required to forgive 3,086,020 times.)

Not only that, God has given us as Christians the ministry of reconciliation (2 Corinthians 5:18), bringing those who are far from God near to him. We are ambassadors of Christ, missionaries, ministers. A missionary loves the people she is called to serve. When they're throwing spears at her head or shooting her Jeep's tires, she knows it's not personal. She knows that her "struggle is not against flesh and blood, but against...*spiritual* forces of evil" (Ephesians 6:12, emphasis mine).

It's the same in a spiritually unequal marriage. Yes, there are personality differences. Yes, there are behavioral problems. Your husband's sloppiness isn't necessarily a spiritual problem. But when his words and actions are spiritual, when the verbal spears are flying, he's still not the enemy. Your real enemy is unseen, and he's just using your husband as his pawn.

When you forget to see the unseen and place blame on the pawn, you tear apart your house, brick by brick. When you do that, you become a pawn too.

Ask God to help you stop your demolition derby and give you new eyes to see. Because—although there are exceptions—most likely your husband's just a regular guy who goes to work, wants his dinner when he comes home, fresh towels and clean sheets, a wife to hold, and kids to play catch with. He wants to provide for his family, find meaning and purpose in his life. He's not a bad guy. He's not your enemy. He's the one whom God has given you for the ministry of reconciliation.

(Re)construction 101

One of the basic roles of a wife is to be a helper-completer. When Adam first saw Eve he said, "This is now bone of my bones and flesh of my flesh; she shall be called 'woman,' for she was taken out of man" (Genesis 2:23). What an awesome thing for him to say! *My wife: a part of me.*

Although his words aren't as poetic as Adam's, Barry always says between the two of us, we make one complete person. How spiritually perceptive of him. Where he lacks, I make up for it, and vice versa. We pool our talents, strengths, and weaknesses and complete each other. That's the way it is in any marriage, or at least the way it should be. Woman was taken from man. That means he's missing a part of himself without her.

In an ideal union, both husband and wife seek their completion from the Lord and then give to each other out of their abundance. In a spiritually unequal marriage, the non-Christian husband's need is that much greater since he doesn't seek God for fulfillment.

What a tremendous opportunity for a believing wife! Her role of helper-completer takes on an even greater privilege: being able to share God's grace and blessings in her life with her husband. When that's your mind-set—my husband needs me to help and complete him—then you count it all joy to do whatever you can for him. Besides, as I've said before, whatever you do for him, you do for Jesus.

One of the best ways to build your house is to build up your husband. Not with phony praise, "buttering up," but with sincere encouragement. Once, as an experiment, I went out to the front yard where Barry was raking leaves and picked up another rake. I just started raking next to him, not saying anything. Then, as if I'd just thought of it, I told him, "I don't think I could do all that you do for our family." Next, I named all the things he did for our girls and me. As I did, he began to stand straighter and lift his head higher. He made some teasing, wise-guy remark about how incredibly fortunate I am to have him, but I knew I had encouraged him—and it was so simple.

Everybody needs encouragement, especially husbands who haven't yet learned to seek the Lord's encouragement for themselves. A wife has the distinctive position of knowing her husband better than anyone else and therefore knowing his precise needs. For some, it's encouragement as a provider. ("Honey, I see the way you work hard for our family and I want you to know I appreciate you.") For others, it could be his appearance or body image. ("I like the way the barber cut your hair this time," or "Let me see you flex your arm muscle!")

Remember, most men hide their insecurities, usually behind bravado. When looking for specific ways to encourage your husband, listen for the "macho" and start there. It could be your husband's way of asking.

Another way of building your house is by keeping up your appearance. In *His Needs, Her Needs,* author Willard Harley Jr. lists the five basic needs of husbands and wives. For women, he says our needs are:

1. affection
2. conversation
3. honesty and openness
4. financial support
5. family commitment

Our husbands need:

1. sexual fulfillment
2. recreational companionship
3. an attractive spouse
4. domestic support
5. admiration

In this day, to talk about appearances seems old-fashioned and archaic. Besides, it's the inner beauty that counts, right? Yes, but let's face it: Men are visual and they appreciate beauty. A man is encouraged when his wife looks her best. Most men don't demand perfection, but they do want to feel comfortable and proud when they're seen with their wives. Often all that's needed are clean clothes and combed hair. It encourages a man to know you care enough to present your best self to him. Don't fool yourself in thinking there isn't some other woman who is willing to step in and take your place either. Chances are, your husband knows of at least one who turns his head and doesn't care that he's married. Barry tells me all the time about the offers he gets. I'm no beauty, but because I'm careful about my appearance, I know my husband is pleased.

Encouraging Him Toward Jesus

The best advice I ever received from a pastor regarding how to encourage an unbelieving husband's steps toward Jesus was this: Leave him wanting more. If he shows any interest and begins to ask questions, give honest answers but refrain from preaching a sermon. (We'll talk more about words in a later chapter.) A simple answer encourages him to ask again.

Along with answering his questions is giving him space to investigate on his own. (And praying like crazy behind the scenes.) This way, you encourage your husband with your trust that he's a big boy who doesn't need to be spoon-fed.

Although I haven't figured out why this is so, I just know that generally it's not a wife's active, obvious ministry that brings a man to Christ, but someone else's. However, of the men I talked with who came to faith in Christ long after their wives did, all of them said they were encouraged more by the way their wives lived their faith than anything else. (There's that 1 Peter 3 thing!)

Keeth Staton, now a church pastor in Florida, once claimed to be an atheist. He says he never missed an opportunity to ridicule his wife's faith. Even so, by the way she didn't push her faith on him, it both drove him nuts and encouraged him to investigate for himself. He says whenever she would go to church, he would pull out a Bible and read.

I have a friend who once found a church bulletin on the seat of her husband's car—from a church sixty miles away. Later he said something to her about the sermon he had heard. My friend said that in a fleeting moment of wisdom she decided to play it smart and stifled the urge to bombard him with questions. (Although she admitted she couldn't disguise her confused delight.)

"I don't remember what I said, but I do remember reacting as if his attending out-of-town churches was a common occurrence," she told me. "For all I know, it might be." Only God knows what goes on in anyone's heart. Still, it's reassuring to know that once the Lord begins to work, we don't have to be there to direct and orchestrate things. Imagine that!

On the other hand, if we provide a safe environment and lots of space, when our husbands take a step toward Jesus, they'll know we won't chase after them and try to get them to leap. Believe me, that's the fastest way to get a man to run the other way.

Unless the Lord Builds the House

"Unless the LORD builds the house," writes the psalmist, "its builders labor in vain. Unless the LORD watches over the city, the watchmen stand guard in vain" (Psalm 127:1). Usually I remember this scripture after I've done some home-wrecking damage: I've taken matters into my own hands, tried to speed up the process or do God's job in Barry's life. My goal is to remember it *before* I start yanking at the shingles.

It helps to remember that the Father is a master architect. He spoke creation into existence with one word. He is the one who builds and designs my house—my family—from the foundation up.

Construction takes time. When I try to help, I get in the way, I "labor in vain." I'm like a Three Stooges film, making a mess, getting hit on the noggin with my own hammer. The Lord builds the house, but that doesn't mean I'm not a part of the process. He gives me an important job to do: to be a helper-completer for my husband, an encourager, a source of refreshment, and a blessings sharer.

With her own hands a foolish woman tears her house down, but with her hands offered to God, she aids the building process by building up her husband. Not because she thinks that will bring him to faith in Christ quicker, but because she knows that's what brings God delight.

THINK ON THESE THINGS

- **Think** about all the ways some women brutally tear down their husbands. We've all seen public displays of disrespect; however, there are other, subtle behaviors that cause damage to a man. List some of them. (Friend, if you've been guilty of some of these, keep in mind that it's never too late to start fresh with the Lord's enabling.)

- **Study** the following scriptures that deal with the concept of "building up":
  Proverbs 31:12
  Matthew 7:1-5
  Galatians 5:22-26
  Ephesians 4:25–5:2
  Ephesians 5:15-16
  Titus 2:4-5

- **Apply** what you've studied by making a list of ways you can build your husband up. Pray and ask the Lord to give you creativity, a willing heart, and lots of opportunities to put his Word into practice.

• **Consider** what Bryan Chapell writes in *Each for the Other:* "When a woman nourishes, nurtures and affirms her spouse, her love for him deepens. The regard she gives her husband not only expresses her love but builds it. When such regard diminishes, love itself fails." We can't nourish from an empty well, however. What is our source? (See Isaiah 40:28-31.)

• "Does my husband know that I protect his reputation by never criticizing him before others? Does he know that even when he fails, I will be there to cushion his fall? Does he know that no matter how harshly he may be treated at work, he can come home to a safe place where he will be loved and appreciated?"

—Susan Hunt, *By Design*

Eight

The Intimate Ally

No pun intended, but sex is a touchy subject for most women. It touches the core of who we are. It touches our soul and our spirit. On the other hand, I've heard it said that all a man requires for a sexual relationship is for his wife to show up. (I heard that from a man, so I'm assuming he speaks for his entire gender, although I also assume there are exceptions.)

Not so with women. Before we're able to even show up, we need that emotional connection first. We need to feel cherished and loved before we can respond physically. We long to be known and understood *first*.

As you well know, that's not so simple when there's a spiritual chasm between you and your husband. Sex isn't simple anymore. As one woman told me, "When I recommitted my life to the Lord, our sex life started to suffer. I don't know if my husband's punishing me—I don't know what's going through his mind because he won't say. Sex is so sporadic, and I've given up on intimate relations. Right now all I do is pray for him and our marriage. There seems to be nothing else I can do."

Another woman said, "I'm torn inside. I love my husband, I really do, but because he's often so antagonistic about my faith, sometimes I'll pretend I'm sleeping if I think he wants sex—especially if he's been out drinking with his friends and comes in late. I hate that I feel this way…but that's the way I feel."

For several other women I talked with, the subject of sex brings intense feelings of anger and pain. "Sex doesn't exist in our home anymore," said one woman, "and I'm perfectly satisfied not to have it because I don't love my husband anymore and just can't perform the act."

She said her husband uses sex as a bargaining tool for his church attendance. ("I'll go to church with you if you'll have sex with me.") Or he uses her refusals as a reason not to go. She's angry, he's angry, and she blames his unbelief as the cause of their sexual (and other) problems.

Although many of the women I talked with for this book considered sex to be repulsive, or tolerable at best, many others smiled when asked for their thoughts. Still, with almost all their answers came a "but."

One stay-at-home mother of two said, "Our sex life is good, when it happens, *but* I long for more intimacy during lovemaking. With my being a Christian, we have so many differences now. I love him with all my heart, *but* sometimes I just wish I could change him into the man I would like him to be. I've even found myself praying during sex. I'm not saying I don't ever enjoy it, or that I do it out of duty, because I don't. *But* since I became a Christian, I just don't feel as close to him as I did before."

Unmet Needs

Cosmopolitan magazine conducted a survey on sexual fulfillment and discovered 70 percent of the women surveyed described their love life as dissatisfying or unrewarding. We could argue that the percentage is so high because a secular magazine conducted the survey and most likely included responses from a high percent of non-Christian women.

A similar survey conducted by *Redbook* magazine found that sixty-two thousand out of the eighty-three thousand women who described themselves as "religious" rated their sexual relationship with their husband as "very satisfying." Many of those also commented that their faith added to a general sense of well-being, which in turn enabled them to enjoy their sexuality.

That may be true, but there are still many Christian women who are not content with their sex lives—even those married to men in ministry, says Christian marriage therapist Melissa McBurney. She says many are repulsed at the thought of sex with their husbands.

Sadly, it's a broad problem, and the reasons are as varied as the women themselves. One common complaint is feeling "used." A woman thinks, *My husband isn't interested in any part of my life; he's cold to me when it comes to my Christianity, but as soon as we get into bed, suddenly he's all over me. He doesn't realize how used I feel when he does that. And if I refuse him, he gets mad and calls me a prude—or worse.*

He's angry. You're angry. He's thinking about his "old" wife, the one you used to be before Jesus came and changed you. You're thinking about a "new" husband, a Christian husband, and you're angry that things aren't as they should be. So you reject your husband's advances because the alternative is too emotionally painful.

"Sex is often the weapon of choice to express such anger because the sexual act requires a vulnerability that encompasses a person's total being," writes Bob Moeller in *For Better, for Worse, for Keeps*. "It exposes who you are in virtually every area of your life. To lie naked next to someone is to allow him or her to know you as no one else does. So to reject your husband or wife sexually is to say, as nothing else can say, 'I reject you.'

"Sex is more a thermometer than a thermostat. It reflects the emotional temperature of a relationship rather than alters it. So when anger…[is] present, the mercury drops dramatically. (Is the use of the word *frigid* an accident?)"

Moeller goes on to say, "When husbands or wives withhold sexual intimacy from each other, they are often saying, 'I don't feel bonded to you. I don't want to go through with this act. We're not close to each other. It's a lie.'"

In *The Marriage Builder,* Larry Crabb asserts that for the Christian, the basic need to be loved and to feel secure in a relationship is fully met in Christ. He says when marriage partners don't seek their fulfillment in Christ and instead turn to each other to satisfy their essential needs, problems develop. Especially in the area of sexuality, these problems can create anger, hurt, and resentment, which tend to inhibit sexual arousal. As he says, it's difficult to feel angry with your spouse and sensual at the same time.

He adds, "It is fair to say that interpersonal problems that inhibit enjoyable sex can be traced to manipulative goals. Communication difficulties, lack of time together and failure to share openly can all be understood as the result of self-centered goals."

The apostle Paul admonished marriage partners that their bodies do not belong to themselves but to each other, and neither partner should hold back sexually from the other except for a mutually agreed upon season of prayer (1 Corinthians 7:1-6). Even so, knowing that and feeling like responding aren't always a reality.

Ideally, this common ownership of bodies is one of unselfish giving. However, I'm guessing this isn't always the case even in the best, most Christ-centered marriages, because we are all basically self-serving and flawed individuals.

Satisfying Sex Begins with a Renewed Mind

As if living within a spiritually unequal marriage doesn't have enough challenges, often when a woman comes to faith in Christ as an adult, she comes to him with years of sexual damage, whether as a result of her own sinful choices or someone else's abuse. Either way, she doesn't enjoy sex as it's meant to be.

More than a marriage manual or a new nightgown or a bedroom-remodeling project, we need to have our minds renewed. It's not uncommon for a woman to have lived for years with a hardened conscience, indulging herself in an active sexual lifestyle, only to be confronted later on with the truth of God's holy design and purpose for sex within marriage.

Now that she's married, now that sex is to be enjoyed as a gift from a loving Father, she can't shake the (false) guilt she feels over her past and continues to feel guilty. Her thinking becomes reversed. *It was wrong when I was single and did it anyway. But now that it's right, I feel guilty. I'm feeling the consequences of my sin—I feel dirty. I wish I could go back! Oh, to be a virgin again and do it right.*

Friend, if that describes you, if you're having trouble enjoying sex with your husband because of a false sense of guilt, keep reminding yourself that you are now a new creation in Christ (2 Corinthians 5:17), without condemnation (Romans 8:1), and the marriage bed is now pure and undefiled (Hebrews 13:4).

Even if you're convinced of your forgiveness in Christ, it's possible that your views of sex may still be warped. It's sinful or dirty. Animalistic. A nuisance. Too holy to share with an unbelieving husband. It's no more than a recreational pastime. A commodity to trade or a reward for your husband's "good" behavior.

Whatever it is that hangs you up and keeps you from experiencing a freedom of expression, the answer starts with renewing your mind. What does *God* say about sex?

Do a study for yourself from such Scripture passages as Proverbs 5:18-19; 1 Corinthians 7; Hebrews 13:4; and the Song of Solomon. I'll give you a hint: When it comes to sexual expression in marriage, God's for it. After all, he commanded us in the first page of his Book to "multiply" (Genesis 1:28, KJV). The sexual union brings forth "life." No wonder the enemy works to pervert or destroy this gift of God to married couples.

He's also for you and wants to free you from your wrong mind-set about one of his most exciting gifts. When you're "transformed by the renewing of your mind," then you'll be able to know what God's will is for you—his "good, pleasing and perfect will" (Romans 12:2)—even when it comes to sex. (For those who suffer serious sexual response problems due to past abuse, please seek help from a qualified Christian counselor. In the meantime, be encouraged. No sin or trauma is too great for the Lord to forgive or redeem. No spirit is too broken for the Lord to make new.)

One of the first steps in renewing the mind when sex is the last thing you want because you harbor anger and resentment is a shift in goals. As Crabb writes, "Shift from manipulating your spouse to meet your needs to ministering to your spouse's needs. When this shift takes place...debilitating emotions slowly give way to compassion and warmth. Why?

1. The goal of ministering cannot be blocked by your spouse. There is therefore no trigger for resentment toward your partner.

2. Fulfilling the goal of ministry depends only on your willingness.

3. The goal of representing the Lord to your spouse is reachable, at least as a basic direction."

As I asked women about what role they thought sex played in their marriage to their unbelieving husbands, one woman told me, "Although I feel we're missing a certain dimension to our sexual relationship, it's still satisfying. I miss the spiritual intimacy we could share, but I have that with my Savior.

"By serving my husband in bed, I'm serving God. That softens my heart, and when my husband sees that I can still enjoy sex even though we have a different belief system, that helps him. I have no reservations with him, and I believe that by keeping him satisfied, he is more open to God through me."

Another woman said she considered sex with her husband a "bedroom ministry." She often prays during their lovemaking that God will use her to communicate his love for her husband through her. In that way, she brings God close—to herself, to her husband, and to the two of them as a couple. She said that keeps her from feeling spiritually distant toward her husband. According to Larry Crabb, when that's a woman's mind-set, she feels useful, not used.

And God says, "It is good."

What Sex Means to a Man

In the previous chapter I mentioned Willard F. Harley Jr.'s list of the five basic needs of husbands and wives in marriage. Sexual fulfillment topped the men's list. That means, if I as a wife want to meet my husband's needs as an act of worship to the Lord, I need to know the importance my husband places on sex.

As Norm Wright explains in *What Men Want*, sex is important to a man, but men want more from sex than just sex. Most men want complete and intimate relationships. He says, "Men do hunger for intimacy, despite the fact that many substitute sex for sharing and emotion."

He says men who confuse emotional needs for sexual needs and think of sex *as* intimacy become frustrated and upset when they don't have a sexual outlet. "Sex," he writes, "is usually their only source of closeness."

That's good news for women, whose number-one need is for affection. A husband's sexual advances, while they may be physiologically driven, are most likely the only way he knows how to reach out for an emotional connection with his wife. I don't know about you, but the more I learn about what makes men tick, the more precious my husband becomes to me. He's not someone to fend off or give in to, but someone who needs my embrace.

Not only does sex satisfy a man's physical and emotional needs, but it also fulfills his manhood, say Tim and Beverly LaHaye in *The Act of Marriage*. Sex makes a man a man in his own eyes and gives him self-confidence. "Genuine love flourishes in giving," they write. "That is why a devoted husband finds great delight in knowing his wife enjoys his lovemaking."

Melissa McBurney suggests that women who are having trouble responding sexually should spend time reminiscing about good (sexual) times with their husbands. (Come on, there has to be one or two!) "Praise him for what a good lover he is and you will be amazed at how his attitudes will soften," says the Colorado-based marriage therapist. "Men, being made in the image of God, love praise and actually thrive on it." However, she cautions, don't let anger get in the way of giving him what he needs so much.

For a man, sex also enhances his love for his wife, according to the LaHayes. "Because a man has been endowed by God with an intense sex drive and a conscience, the satisfactory release of that drive without provoking his conscience will enhance his love for the person who makes that possible."

Only a wife can do that, they add. "Because sex is such a necessary

part of a man's life and married love preserves the innocence of his conscience, the woman who provides these for him will increasingly become
the object of his love."

While it's true that some men (and women) can harden their hearts
and block out the voice of their consciences, others genuinely want to
do the right things for their wives and families. So when it comes to sex,
a woman who desires to keep her family together does herself a favor
when she responds positively to her husband.

"A sexually satisfied man is usually a contented man," the LaHayes
write. While this won't solve major problems, it does tend to reduce
minor irritations.

Maybe even put smiles on both partners' faces.

This Is My Beloved, and This Is My Friend

Number two on Willard Harley's list of a man's needs in marriage is
recreational companionship. Doing stuff together. Women like to sit
and chat, "do lunch," go for walks. Guys like to do stuff. They fish,
hunt, shoot hoops, watch a ball game, whittle. They sit side by side,
sometimes not even talking, yet as long as there's some type of activity
going on, they're building a friendship.

Ideally, a husband and wife should be each other's best friend.
Maybe you and your husband are still friends. Maybe the two of you
never were friends. Maybe you were before Christ came into your life,
but now you've gone your separate ways and developed new friendships
outside the marriage.

Maybe you're thinking, *First she says I should have sex with him—
now she's saying I have to be his friend, too? Is there no limit to my sacrifice?*

In Christ there is no limit. So, to answer your question, yes, you
have to be his friend, too. Think of it this way: As you cultivate a

friendship with your husband, and the more fun you have together, the closer you'll become. (Can I hear a "Duh"?) The closer you become, the more relaxed you'll be around each other. When you're relaxed and enjoying each other's company, you're no longer a threat to each other. He doesn't feel like prey for your Christian conquest, and he's no longer the Big Bad Enemy. You're simply married friends doing stuff together.

Fun is important to any marriage but especially in a spiritually unequal one. "If we neglect this and do not make time to be together regularly where we can enjoy each other's company, we not only put the relationship at risk, but also make it harder for an unbelieving spouse to come to faith," says Michael Fanstone in *Unbelieving Husbands and the Wives Who Love Them.* "A husband who is not yet committed to Christ is likely to be more open to his wife's faith if their relationship is fresh and vibrant."

If the thought of friendship with your husband seems an impossibility right now, that's not necessarily a bad thing. That just gives God that much greater an opportunity to work in your relationship. However, if you've been following everything written in previous chapters and have opened yourself up to renewing your mind, then chances are you'll be open to this, too.

Where do you start? As with everything, start with prayer. Ask God to give you a heart of friendship toward your husband. Then go slow. You don't want to scare him away or cause him to think this is a gimmick or a ploy to spring Jesus on him. Your goal is oneness and connection, doing everything as unto the Lord.

Next, ask the Lord to help you think of fun, nonthreatening activities for the two of you to enjoy together. Here's a list of ideas to get you started:

1. Jump on a trampoline together.
2. Plant a garden.
3. Go for a drive.

4. Visit a museum.

5. Plan a trip (even if it's only imaginary).

6. Daydream together.

7. Volunteer together.

8. Develop a common hobby.

9. Explore a flea market.

10. Refinish a piece of furniture together.

11. Play Scrabble.

12. Visit an amusement park.

13. Roller-skate.

14. Ride bikes.

15. Build a bonfire.

16. Go swimming in a secluded place.

17. Fish from a pier.

18. Cook together.

19. Take a bus tour.

20. Join a gym and work out together.

21. Spread out a blanket and watch the night sky.

22. Learn a foreign language.

23. Take pictures.

24. Toss a Frisbee.

25. Shoot hoops.

26. Ride horses.

27. Go canoeing.

28. Pick berries.

29. Go to a ball game (even Little League).

30. Try a new food (sushi, Mexican, Thai, etc.).

I can't promise that your life will be easy if you cultivate a friendship with your husband, but it will be easier. I especially can't promise a sure-fire, five-step plan for great sex. All I can promise is that God is for you and he will equip and enable you to be a vessel of his love and grace to the one he's given you.

My prayer for you is that you will know God's pleasure as you seek to honor him and that you'll know that you can do even that which you think is an impossibility.

After all, with God, nothing, nothing, *nothing* is impossible.

Just wait and see.

THINK ON THESE THINGS

- **Think** about this almost scandalous statement from author Kathy Peel: "Prayer and sex are words seldom used in the same sentence. But they should be." How could prayer affect a woman's sexual relationship with her unbelieving husband?

- **Study** what God has to say about sex in marriage:
  Genesis 1:28
  Genesis 2:24-25
  Genesis 24:67; 2 Samuel 12:24
  Deuteronomy 24:5
  1 Corinthians 7:3-5
  Song of Solomon (preferably in a modern translation or paraphrase)

- **Apply** these scriptures. (That's the fun part!) But first, what have you discovered about how God feels about sex? How does your view line up with God's Word? If you're still struggling in this area with wrong ideas or guilt, consider talking to a counselor. But talk to God first—and talk to your husband.

• **Consider** how your sexual relationship with your unbelieving husband can be a "bedroom ministry," as some women have called it. If this is one area that has been less than satisfying, pray and ask God to give you a heart for this "ministry" and to increase your capacity to both give and receive pleasure.

• "Sex is too important to marriage to assume it is merely a symptom that will take care of itself when other problems are solved. That is not true. Sex is a building block for constructing and maintaining a solid, happy marriage. A good sexual relationship can keep a marriage together when a lot of other things are shaky."

—LeeAnn Smucker Rawlins, *Loving for Life*

Nine

Me and
My Big Mouth

*H*is name was George and he had a big mouth. You could tell him anything and he'd blab it. He belonged to my mother and sat perched in a black wrought-iron cage near her kitchen. As parrots go, George was average, I suppose. I'm not a parrot fan, but I started warming up to George when I realized his gift of gab.

When we moved from Maine to California, we stayed with my parents while we looked for a place to live. I had been a Christian only a year or two and hadn't yet learned that God didn't need my help in running the universe, especially as it pertained to Barry's faith life.

At the time, I considered meeting George a serendipitous experience. Since Barry had made it known that my gospel babblings and nonstop preaching at him was turning him off, I decided to keep my mouth shut. After all, 1 Peter 3:1 does tell wives to zip their lips.

It never mentions feeding words to a parrot.

So that's what I did. After my parents and Barry all left the house in the mornings, I'd sit down next to George and say, "Jesus loves you!" "Come to Jesus!" "Repent and be baptized!"

It didn't work. All George would spout was standard parrot fare: "Pretty bird" and "Hi, George." Thanks to my youngest brother, he knew a few saltier phrases as well. But the bird wouldn't cooperate as my gospel mouthpiece.

Too bad, because I had it planned brilliantly. As soon as George uttered something spiritual and profound, I would feign surprise and cry, "Look! Even God's creatures praise him!" Then Barry would be convicted to the core of his being because even a stupid bird like George knew enough to praise the Lord. After that, I could rejoice and say, "I told you so," and I would live happily ever after.

Not a holy squawk out of him. It was as if God kept the bird's mouth closed on purpose, which frustrated me to no end. If Barry wouldn't listen to me and he couldn't listen to George, then how would he hear the gospel?

For the longest time, this remained a mystery to me. *But Lord, who else knows what pushes his buttons? Who knows what scriptures he needs to hear? Who knows his sins and his faults better than I do? Who better than I to point them out?*

The truth is, outside of God himself, I am probably the one who knows my husband best. However, for whatever reason, God instructs, tells, commands wives to live out their faith quietly before their husbands. That means no preaching, no teaching. No spiritual monologues or trying to get birds to do the talking for you.

No coaxing your kids either. It's one thing to have a child ask on her own, "Daddy, why don't you go to church too?" But training your preschooler to say it is manipulation and will most likely come back and bite you. At best it will be ineffective.

Peter's Lip-Zip Principle

You probably know this passage of Scripture by heart. (Or if you don't, then you should.) In 1 Peter 3:1-4 God instructs married women:

> Wives…be submissive to your husbands so that, if any of
> them do not believe the word, *they may be won over with-*
> *out words* by the behavior of their wives, when they see
> the purity and reverence of your lives. Your beauty…
> should be that of your inner self, the unfading beauty of
> a gentle and quiet spirit, *which is of great worth in God's*
> *sight.* (emphasis mine)

That phrase "won over without words" literally means "won over without words," as in "no words." Lip zipped. Quit your babbling. That's not to say there aren't times to speak. Peter also writes that believers should "always be prepared to give an answer to everyone who asks you to give the reason for the hope that [we] have" (1 Peter 3:15). He cautions, "But do this with gentleness and respect." That means giving simple answers, not rambling dissertations.

We women love to talk and hash things out, and we think men are the same way, but they're not. Men generally aren't good with too many words. When they reach their capacity, they tune out. Still, Barry and I have had some great spiritual discussions, but rarely because I've instigated them. Those times generally lead to arguments and frustration on both our parts.

I have noticed, however, that since I've adopted the zipped-lip approach as my usual way of living with my husband, spiritual conversations are more welcome on his part and less forced on mine. I like to think it's because Barry's being won over by my actions. As the adage goes, actions speak louder than words. And our actions, our lives, are to be quiet and gentle.

That's what pleases God.

"Shhhhhhh!"

So there's no misunderstanding, let's define the meaning of a gentle and quiet spirit, especially as it applies to a spiritually mismatched marriage.

First of all, a person's spirit is her essence, who she really is. My spirit encompasses all my thoughts and personality; it's the quality that makes me *me*. It's that part of me that connects with God and with others.

A gentle spirit then is one that is refined, not rough or harsh. It's courteous and generous, tame and gracious. It's calm and calming, mellow and tender. A woman with a gentle spirit is a delight to be around. She's a soft breeze on a warm day, a cold glass of lemonade, a soft kiss. A mother rocking her child.

A woman with a gentle spirit isn't a pushover or a doormat, neither is she bland or boring. She can have fun—she should have fun—and still possess a gentle spirit.

From a prison cell the apostle Paul wrote, "Let your gentleness be evident to all" (Philippians 4:5). He added, the Lord is close by, so don't be worried and anxious. Tell God what's troubling you, pray about what you need, and the most unbelievable peace that only comes from the hand of a loving, almighty Father will guard your heart and your mind and calm your spirit. Your life circumstances may be in chaos, but you, my friend, will be just fine.

Not only that, but the Father will give you a gentle spirit, that you may be a calming influence to those around you (Philippians 4:6-7, my paraphrase).

A quiet spirit is similar. Whereas gentleness involves actions, quietness refers more to the inward state of being. A quiet spirit is one that's not in turmoil or easily excitable; it doesn't fret. A woman with a quiet spirit isn't showy or pushy because of insecurity. She's unruffled, trusting, still, tranquil. "The fruit of righteousness will be peace," says the prophet Isaiah. "The effect of righteousness will be quietness and confidence forever" (Isaiah 32:17).

I always say it's easy to be married when you're not. When you're single, you imagine yourself handling any number of situations with an imaginary husband, and in all of them you're always gentle and quiet. But in real life, when your husband brings home a stack of slasher movies and a bottle of tequila and wants you to join him, or when he starts in on how "all churches are filled with hypocrites," you feel your blood pressure rise and your spirit become *dis*quieted. You want to grab your husband and shake salvation into him.

But you know, of course, that you can't.

So what do you do when you feel you can't be quiet? When you feel anything but gentle and you want to pound last Sunday's sermon into his thick skull? "Do not fear," writes Zephaniah, "do not let your hands hang limp. The LORD your God is with you, he is mighty to save. He will take great delight in you, *he will quiet you with his love*" (Zephaniah 3:16-17, emphasis mine).

God quiets us with his love. He whispers, "I'm here. I'm in control. I'm holding on to you and won't let go." When we know that, our spirit quiets and we're able to respond in gentleness.

And that speaks volumes.

The Taming of the Tongue

Oh, that tongue! Such a small hunk of flesh, yet capable of so much destruction. You have a fight with your husband, and he calls you a blank-blank Jesus Freak. Or he throws your Bible across the room, or maybe just sets his cup of coffee on top of it. Immediately you retaliate: "I wish I never married you." "You're such a loser." "You make me sick." "If you were a real man, you'd take the lead in our family."

The New Testament writer James says, "By our speech we can ruin the world, turn harmony to chaos, throw mud on a reputation, send the whole world up in smoke and go up in smoke with it, smoke right from the pit of hell" (James 3:6, MSG).

Solomon said, "A fool's mouth is his ruin, and his lips are the snare of his soul" (Proverbs 18:7, NASB).

But you know all that. You know that all it takes is a half-dozen thoughtless words to ruin a moment or even destroy an entire relationship for a lifetime. When the Bible talks about the power of the tongue, it talks in extremes: life and death, healing and calamity. It calls the tongue a fire and a world of evil. Reckless words are said to pierce like a sword; harsh words stir up strife.

On the other hand, the tongue brings healing, and a gentle answer turns away wrath. A soothing tongue is a tree of life. Pleasant words are a honeycomb.

Again, you know all that. You read it in your Bible and live it every day. But knowing the good and right thing and doing it are two separate issues. I know I have trouble with my tongue. Toothpaste and mouthwash just don't do the trick when it comes to taming it.

A few years ago I attended a Bible study on the book of Galatians in which the leader gave us an assignment. She called it a "tongue exercise." For one week we were not to:

- gossip or spread a bad report
- complain
- criticize

- blameshift or make excuses
- boast
- deceive others

Instead, we were to:

- share the gospel with others
- affirm others
- express gratitude and praise
- apologize quickly
- speak directly and honestly to everyone

I lasted about two seconds. The first words out of my mouth were "Oh, man! I can't do that!" That was the point of the exercise: Short of wiring our jaws shut, you and I *can't* tame our tongues by trying, even with the best of intentions. That's why, even when you've psyched yourself up and vowed that you weren't going to be critical and naggy to your husband anymore, as soon as he does or says something you consider "ungodly," you berate him. Or you keep quiet, but then when he's out of earshot you call your best friend and complain. Or when he asks you about the checkbook entry marked T.B.B., you tell him it's The Bread Bakery and not The Bible Bookstore.

It's not the tongue that's the problem—it's our hearts. Jesus said the words we speak reflect what's in our hearts (Matthew 12:34). So if we fill our hearts with thoughts of bitterness and complaint, worry, blame, and self-righteousness, that's the well we draw from.

What's the answer? It's not in trying harder. As with any bad habit, pet sin, stronghold—whatever you call it—trying harder rarely works. Instead, the remedy is always *replacement*, which begins with *returning*. We return to the Cross and remain there until we see our sin as God sees it, owning it for ourselves, then beholding his grace. As grace replaces all the heart-stuff that taints our words, our words become gracious. Grace-full.

But that's just the start. The heart has a way of returning to what it's used to, and sadly, it's used to sin. It's a constant battle but one in which Christ battles for us and with us, not against us. Still, it's up to me and it's up to you to fill our minds with whatever is true, noble, right, pure, lovely, or admirable, as the apostle Paul wrote *while he was in prison and in chains* (Philippians 4:8).

When our minds are filled with beauty and grace, so will be our words. When our words are gracious, we'll be easier to live with. If we're easier to live with, our husbands will notice. A woman named Penny told me her long-distance truckdriver husband says she seems happier and is a lot nicer to be around when she's been to church. "He won't go with me, but if he's out on the road on a Saturday, he'll call home and remind me to go to church on Sunday."

Another woman, Cathy, concentrates on what she likes about her husband. That way, when things get tense, she has a well of good thoughts to draw upon. She said sometimes she'll open her mouth to pick or nag and out will pop something kind.

As both Cathy and Penny have discovered, it truly is from the overflow of our hearts that the mouth speaks.

As for the Rest of the Body...

Right about now you're probably looking for a loophole. An exception. *That's all fine and dandy, but I've got messages to get across, and if I can't use my tongue...well, there are other ways, you know.*

How about:

- A martyred sigh as you get yourself and the kids dressed for church. ("That's okay. You stay in bed. I will endure. This is my cross, and I bear it with joy." Grunt, grunt, sigh.)

- A narrowing of the eyes at your husband's swearing, beer drinking, smoking, etc. ("You godless heathen. I'm *so* past that.")

- The icicle shoulder or loud silent treatment. ("You want me to keep quiet? I'll show you quiet.")

- Keeping your distance. ("I don't want any of your unbelief to rub off on me.")

As with our tongues, our nonverbal communication—which often speaks louder than words because we can fake our speech but not our attitudes—is a heart problem. The remedy is the same as with our words. Take care of the heart, and the rest will follow.

Friend, here's what you do: Next time you're alone and you have some time, ask God to show you your body language. As you do, remember: God is for you. He wants to transform you into a pleasure to be around and turn you into a wife with a quiet and gentle spirit. As he begins to reveal and do his work in you, I promise you he won't condemn you; he only wants to heal and help you communicate with the husband he's given you to love. So let him, won't you?

How About Those Yankees?

You may be thinking all that's left to say to your husband is sugary Barbie-doll platitudes. "Have a nice day, dear." "May I rub your feet, dear?" "My, my, but you're looking manly tonight, dear." *Oh, gag me.*

More than anything, I think husbands want wives who are real and authentic. They want someone to shoot the breeze with, spar with over politics, talk with about those Yankees or Bucs or Pistons. They want someone they can bounce ideas off of without the threat of a lecture or sermon or "well-placed" Bible verse. It's possible to carry on a godly, grace-filled conversation without mentioning the name of Jesus. If your life is full of Jesus, your whole being will communicate it—even while talking about mulching the flower beds out back.

You might be surprised at just how much Jesus is communicated that way. "Let your light shine before men," Jesus told his disciples, "that they may see your good deeds and praise your Father in heaven" (Matthew 5:16).

So if you're at a point where your conversation with your husband is stiff and stilted or even a battlefield because you've tried to inject Jesus at every opportunity, it may be time to concentrate on other topics for discussion. Your light will still shine, and chances are your husband will see it better if he's not blindsided by your words.

It also helps to know what men want in a conversation. In *What Makes a Man Feel Loved,* Bob Barnes uses Florence Littauer's list of what men and women want in conversations with each other. Men want:

- Sincerity ("Don't play games or beat around the bush. Tell it to me straight.")

- Simplicity ("Get to the point. Save the details and meanderings for your girlfriends.")

- Sensitivity ("There's a right time and place for everything—and it's usually not when I'm at work or in front of my friends.")

- Stability ("I'm afraid of losing control and being emasculated in front of you.")

Women want:

- Attention ("Please put down the newspaper; this is important to me.")

- Agreement ("I want to find something we agree on, don't you think so too?")

- Appreciation ("Am I important to you?")

- Appointments ("We need to talk. Can we go out for coffee this Saturday morning?")

There's nothing wrong with letting your husband know your communication wants. In fact, most men appreciate being clued in. Just tell him straight out, "Honey, women aren't like men. When women talk, we want _____." You just might open up a whole new avenue of communication as the two of you discover what makes each other tick.

A Word About Grace Sandwiches

Even in the best marriages, times come when partners need to confront one another. It's rarely easy, and in an unequal faith situation, the spiritual imbalance adds a difficult dimension. *Should I say something about his behavior or let God convict him? If I do say something, how do I make sure I'm addressing the behavior and not his person? What if I drive him further away from the Lord with my words?*

I had a Christian friend who sat back and watched as her unbelieving husband went out drinking with his buddies regularly. He would come home at 3 A.M. on Saturdays or Sundays, and she didn't say a word to him. After nearly ten years of him showing no signs of changing, she decided she had to say something to him.

One day, as they sat together on their front porch, she told him, "I love you. But I don't like that you stay out so late drinking with your friends. I miss you."

She said her husband was shocked. Because she had never said anything, he thought she didn't care. He stopped staying out late and eventually stopped going out regularly with his buddies. He's still not a Christian, but he enjoys being with his wife.

My friend could have handled it differently. She could have reached a point where she'd had enough and just ripped into her husband, unloading a decade's worth of hurt and anger. But she didn't. She gave her husband what I call a "grace sandwich" by surrounding her message—I don't want you out drinking anymore—with grace. She began with "I love you" and ended it with "I miss you."

Another friend recently told me about a situation in which her husband made a joking comment to their teenage daughter and her boyfriend about the three of them drinking beer together. My friend struggled over that for a few days until she knew she couldn't let it go, but she also knew she had to handle it with grace. So she waited until her husband was alone, then told him, "I know you were just having fun with the kids about drinking beer together and didn't mean it. But it made you look foolish, and you're not a fool."

He made light of it, but that's not her responsibility. She knew she had to speak to him—without calling him a jerk or accusing him of being a bad role model. She simply couched it in grace, pointed out that one instance, then let it drop.

If you notice, that's how God speaks to us. He tells us he loves us, points out a specific sin ("You lied," not "You're a bad person"), then gives us a word of encouragement so we will go forward once we've been forgiven.

He feeds us grace sandwiches. Likewise, he gives us all the ingredients necessary to feed them to those around us, especially to our husbands, who are particularly hungry for such a meal.

THINK ON THESE THINGS

- **Think** about your speech during the past twenty-four hours. How many of your words were uplifting, encouraging, pleasant, loving, necessary, or helpful? How many do you wish you could take back?

- **Study** what the Bible says about our speech and the power of words. Using a concordance (look up "tongue," "lips," "words," "speak," and "mouth"), make a list of verses that talk about helpful speech and destructive speech. Make a chart and refer to it daily.

- **Apply** what you've written down to your own speech. In her book *Words That Hurt, Words That Heal*, author Carole Mayhall recommends processing our words through the list of characteristics found in James 3:17: Are our words pure, gentle, peaceable, full of mercy and good fruit, unwavering, without hypocrisy? What is the real problem when it comes to our words? (See Matthew 12:33-37 and Jeremiah 17:9.) What is our best remedy? (See 1 John 1:9.)

- **Consider** the women at your church who exhibit the "gentle and quiet spirit" 1 Peter 3:1-4 talks about. Note their nonverbal communication as well as the way they speak to their husbands and to others. Pray and ask the Lord to develop that quality in you—and then take note of your progress.

- "We women would do well to ponder more so that our words flow from our worship. So often we are quick to speak what is on our minds, especially to men, and the proliferation of our own words often moves us away from, instead of closer to, the words God wants to speak to us. Are we willing to listen to God's voice so that what we speak comes only from what he is whispering in our ear?"

    —Nancy Groom, *Heart to Heart About Men*

Lord, Hear My Prayer

D^{ear God,}

In case you haven't noticed, I've been really good lately. I've waited patiently for nearly a month now for you to save my husband, and while I haven't seen any changes in him, now would be an ideal time. It's almost my birthday—you could make him a Christian as a birthday present for me. That's a great idea, don't you think?

I promise I'll read the Bible twice a day if you'll answer my prayer! I'll give to the food pantry and go without ice cream for a year and even volunteer in the nursery. (You know what a sacrifice that would be.)

Lord, I think you should answer this because it would glorify you to have both of us in agreement on spiritual things. Not to mention it would make my life a whole lot easier. Don't you think you owe it to yourself to have both of us serving you?

Jesus said we could ask anything in his name and we could have it. So in Jesus' name I'm asking for my husband to (1) come to faith in Christ, (2) take me to the marriage conference next month, (3) fix the switch for the dining room light, and (4) stop throwing his dirty socks behind the couch.

I'm claiming this, Lord. I have all faith. Big faith. I know you can do this! That you WILL do this. I can picture it now. My friends are all pray- ing too. We're agreeing together that this is going to happen. That it's already happened.

Please, Lord? Please? I'll be good, I promise. And I won't bother you again, if you'll just answer this one request of mine.

In Jesus' name. Amen.

If you're reading this book, chances are you've prayed that prayer or one that's similar. When you live with a never-believing or a once-professing husband, that prayer mirrors your heart, doesn't it? You want relief from a hard situation, you offer God bargains if he'll grant your wish, you employ every catch phrase or tip on the market in a desperate attempt to get your prayers answered.

Well-meaning people come up to you at church and say, "Honey, you just gotta pray that husband of yours into the kingdom." They give advice: "Pray in Jesus' name." "Pick out a promise in the Bible and claim it."

They offer their own testimony: "My grandmother prayed Ezekiel 36:26 for my grandfather every day for forty years, and that's what finally did it."

They tell you to keep praying and never give up.

So you go home and pray and pray and pray. With feeling and faith and gusto. But…he remains unsaved and seems perfectly content to stay that way. And you wonder, if prayer changes things, why am I not see- ing any changes? And if God already knows what he's going to do any- way and has all power and authority to do it, what purpose does praying serve? And if I don't pray, will God still act? Can my prayers really effect change? Can I twist God's arm?

From Prayer Wimp to Prayer Warrior

Even though I wrote a book a few years ago on the subject of prayer and the kinds of prayers God always answers, I still don't fully understand it. I do know that God's people have always been a people of prayer. I know that God hears the cries and prayers of his people and he answers their requests. But I also know his answers aren't always what we expect.

I've known people who pray with great faith for people to be healed, but they're not. I've prayed weak, doubting prayers for myself or someone else, and they've been answered. In either case, I'm left scratching my head, still confused about the purpose of prayer—especially as it pertains to praying for a husband's salvation. Why are one woman's prayers answered immediately and others' not?

It seems when it comes to prayer, I often have more questions than answers.

Even so, I do know prayer isn't:

- A magic formula. "Say these words three times a day for thirty days—with a money-back guarantee if not completely satisfied."

- An obligation for God to answer. "Lord, you said 'Ask and it will be given to you.' Well, I'm asking, so you have to give!"

- A way of changing God's mind. If my prayers had the power to do that, then God wouldn't be almighty.

- Dependent on the amount of my faith. Jesus said those who have faith as tiny as a mustard seed can tell a mulberry tree to be uprooted and throw itself into the sea and it will.

- A last resort. "Oh, well. Nothing else is working—I might as well give praying a try."

Instead, prayer is:

- God's will for us. "Be joyful always; *pray continually*; give thanks in all circumstances, for this is God's will for you in Christ Jesus" (1 Thessalonians 5:16-18, emphasis mine).

- A privilege. We are invited to approach God's throne with boldness and confidence (Hebrews 4:16), as much-loved children (1 John 3:1).

- An effective weapon against an unseen enemy. John Bunyan said, "Prayer is a shield to the soul, a sacrifice to God and a scourge to Satan."

- A means of communicating our fretful hearts to a loving Father. "Trust in him at all times, O people; pour out your hearts to him, for God is our refuge" (Psalm 62:8).

- A lifeline between us and God and a vehicle of his peace in our lives. "Do not be anxious about anything, but in everything, by prayer and petition, with thanksgiving, present your requests to God. And the peace of God, which transcends all understanding, will guard your hearts and your minds in Christ Jesus" (Philippians 4:6-7).

So why pray? Because the Father said we could...and also that we should.

If Prayer Changes Things...Then, Lord, Change My Husband!

Let's be honest. Often a woman's motivation in praying for her husband is because she wants him to change so her life will be easier. *If he were a Christian, I wouldn't have to endure an inner struggle every Sunday morning regarding going to church. I could put as much money in the offering as I wanted and hang a scripture-etched door knocker on the front door without worrying about World War III erupting.*

A woman named Colleen says, "My prayers tend to be, 'I put up with so much; he's so mean and never appreciates anything I do.' I'm usually not interested in improving *me,* only my husband. Anything he tells me I need to change I reject because all I can see is how awful he is. I know I could really glorify God...if only he'd change my husband!"

Unfortunately for our self-serving motives, God knows what brings him the most glory, and obviously it involves keeping some spiritually unequal marriages the way they are—and changing us instead.

I can only speak for myself, but I have a hunch this is true for us all: As God changes me through prayer, my husband also changes. Sometimes in big ways, most often in small ways.

So how does prayer change me?

I'm changed when...I'm faced with my inability to control my situation. *Well, what do you know—I'm not God.* Prayer increases my dependence on the Lord for everything: wisdom, patience, endurance, strength, joy, peace. You name it, I can pray about it. The greater my dependence, the more grateful I am for God's provision. My grateful heart produces a calmness and enthusiasm for living that's evident—and my husband sees. Not only does he see, but he also recognizes the Source of my gratitude.

I'm changed when...through prayer, I focus on my own sin and shortcomings and not my husband's. As Jesus pointed out to his disciples, "Why do you look at the speck of sawdust in your brother's eye and pay no attention to the plank in your own eye?" (Matthew 7:3). When I see my own sin, I'm more apt to show compassion instead of self-righteous judgment toward my husband. We're both sinners.

I'm changed when…I cast all my cares and anxieties on the Lord and he absorbs them and gives me his peace. It's easy to forget that God has everything in his sovereign care and that nothing is too hard for him. As long as your husband is alive, there's hope for his soul. Sometimes we get consumed with what-if and start to worry and fear. But as we pray and pour out our hearts to God who is our comfort, he reassures us that nothing is out of his hand. We pray until we're calm and quiet.

I'm also changed when…I see glimpses of his workings in my husband's life. One woman told me that her husband travels during the week and she tends to get discouraged when she doesn't see any spiritual progress. One Sunday afternoon, as her husband was preparing to leave for the week, she felt particularly discouraged and pleaded with the Lord, "Please show me something—anything—to encourage me that you're working in John's life!"

About five minutes later her husband said, "Oh by the way, in case you call me on a Wednesday night and I don't answer, I might be at this church down the street."

She said she did a double take, laughed, and blurted out, "But you don't go to church!" Then she remembered he had been telling her about a certain church near one of his work sites, but at the time she didn't think anything of it.

"I didn't think he'd ever go—I still don't think he ever has," she said. "Actually, whether or not he ever goes to that church is almost secondary. God answered my prayer to be encouraged. He showed me he's doing something. That he's able. He's able to work in my husband's life even when I'm not there to direct and help!"

God's answers, his encouragement, changes me—it changes you—and when we're changed, we're more joyful and peaceful, more secure, more confident in God's ability to change a human heart. After all, if he can change us, he can change anybody.

How Then Should I Pray?

From my own experience and that of other women in spiritually unequal marriages, I've learned the most effective prayer help is found in the Word of God itself. "Praying the Scriptures back to God" some call it. It's taking a passage of Scripture and personalizing it until it speaks to your heart's most desperate needs.

In their book *Praying the Bible for Your Marriage,* David and Heather Kopp write about the tremendous power in praying God's truths back to him. They say that when we use Scripture as the basis of our prayers we:

- Remind ourselves what God has said, including his promises.

- Avoid the trap of "praying the same old thing."

- Come to a more complete understanding of who God is and how he works in our lives.

- Openly agree with God's truth, allowing it to change us and those we love.

- Are rescued from our human limitations. "Claiming Bible truths keeps us from reducing God to our own small human expectations," they write.

- Shift the focus of our prayer from human needs and feelings to God's character, his promises, his past faithfulness, his goodness, and even his extravagances with us.

- Are assured that our prayers lie within and affirm God's will.

As you pray the Scriptures for your husband, you might choose a passage such as Isaiah 65:1, which says, "I revealed myself to those who did not ask for me; I was found by those who did not seek me."

Next, as you begin to pray, you might personalize it by saying, "Lord, you revealed yourself to those who didn't seek you; they weren't interested in you—probably weren't aware of their need for you. While I don't know my husband's heart, from what I can see, he doesn't appear to be seeking you. So I pray that, in your mercy, you will reveal yourself to him in such a way that he can't doubt that it's you."

Likewise, a favorite passage of my friend Mary Ann for her now-Christian husband was always Ezekiel 36:26, which says, "I will give you a new heart and put a new spirit in you; I will remove from you your heart of stone and give you a heart of flesh."

She said as she began to pray this scripture and ask God to remove her husband's heart of stone and replace it with one that was soft and pliable and open toward him, God answered. Not long after she began praying that, her husband's heart did begin to soften toward the Lord and toward her.

Does that mean if you pray that same scripture for your husband he'll be on his knees in a week? Is God obligated to answer, or will he answer quicker if you use his words rather than your own?

No. Never is God obligated to do anything for us, *even* if we use his own words when we pray. However, I do think he is delighted when his children search the Scriptures to discover his heart toward us as well as toward our unbelieving husbands. I think it pleases him to hear us remind him of what he has said. Not so we can hold him to it, but to encourage our own hearts as to his goodness and mercy.

A word of caution: Although the Bible contains many general promises that we can believe with confidence, I think we presume too much to take any old promise that strikes our fancy and "claim" it for our own situation. Even if we believe it with all our heart and get others to believe it for us, often this is nothing more than wishful thinking. Then when the "promise" goes unfulfilled, we're left disappointed and angry at God. *But you promised if I asked for anything in your name, Lord, I would have what I've asked for. I asked that my husband would come to the Sweetheart Dinner, but he refused. You let me down, Lord!*

Oh, we might not say that out loud, but we think it. Friend, we should incorporate God's Word and his promises in our prayers, but we need to be careful to take the entire counsel of Scripture into consideration and not pick and choose what we want to believe for ourselves.

In addition to praying the Scriptures, we can also pray God's name, as my friend Karen likes to do. She takes an aspect of God's character or personality or one of his names in the Bible and uses that as the basis of her prayers. For example, she might choose "God our righteousness." Then as she prays for her husband, she might say, "Lord, my husband is a good man, but he needs to know that his righteousness will never earn him entrance into your kingdom. I pray that you will tell that to his heart. That when he thinks he's good compared to the next guy, you'll show him that he'll never be good compared to Jesus."

Karen says this is a great comfort when praying for herself as well. She pinpoints her need ("I'm lonely and frustrated going to church without my husband") and remembers "Your Maker is your husband" (Isaiah 54:5). When praying for her husband, she'll discern his need and then determine how God alone fulfills it.

A woman named Julie said when she prays for people's salvation, she often asks God to show them their sin and their need for a Savior.

"That's one prayer that always seems to get answered," she said. "Several members of my family have been arrested for driving drunk after I prayed for them specifically. When my husband found out I had prayed, he got scared. Now when he wants to go out with his friends he'll say, 'Please don't pray for me tonight!' Even that I see as an answer to prayer."

We can also pray for:

- Conviction of sin and for godly sorrow that brings repentance and leads to salvation (2 Corinthians 7:10).

- Direction. That whether he turns to the right or to the left, he will hear God's voice behind him saying, "This is the way; walk in it" (Isaiah 30:21).

- Dissatisfaction in anything other than Jesus.

- A hunger and thirst for righteousness.

- That any religious lies he currently believes will be exposed when compared to the truth of God's Word.

- Likewise, that anything he's trusting in, such as his own good works, he will see as empty.

A sample prayer might be:

Father,
You say that my husband is set apart for your special attention
because of his union with me. Thank you, Lord, that I can come
to you and pray on his behalf. Holy is your name! I pray that
your heavenly plan will come to pass in his life. Thank you for

providing all our needs each day, so that my husband will see your blessing on our lives because of your presence in our home. Forgive us when we offend you. Help me to forgive him when he offends me. Keep temptation far from him and protect him from the evil one. My heart's desire is for our family to live in your kingdom, by your power, for your glory forever. Amen.

A Quick Word About Fasting

In addition to prayer, sometimes God may call us to fast; sometimes we may choose to do it on our own. Either way, the Bible speaks of it, and it's a great spiritual discipline. It clears the mind and sharpens our focus. It increases our awareness of our need for God.

In his book *A Hunger for God,* John Piper says fasting helps when we yearn, ache, or mourn. That's what Esther did when she heard the news that the entire nation of Israel was about to be destroyed and it was up to her to seek the mercy of God through her pagan husband, King Xerxes.

Piper also says fasting must be God-ordained and accompanied by prayer and Bible study. Wrong reasons to fast are to lose weight, to attempt to make myself holier or become more virtuous, or to bargain with God.

I've only fasted once with the right motives (I generally think about losing weight), and that was unintentional. I had been going through some powerful spiritual battles, which were so intense I couldn't eat even if I had wanted to. All I could do was cry out to God and pray.

After a week, a powerful climax to the battle occurred when I cast an evil presence out of my house. Looking back, I can see now that it was as Jesus had told his disciples: some evil can only come out by prayer and fasting (Mark 9:29, KJV). At the time, though, all I knew was that I could not eat.

Whether or not you choose to fast, do it prayerfully and purposefully. Look to the scriptural examples of those who fasted, such as Nehemiah, Esther, Moses, Daniel, and Elijah. Above all, do it for the glory of God.

For further reading:

- *A Hunger for God* by John Piper
- *Celebration of Discipline* by Richard Foster
- *Spirit of the Disciplines* by Dallas Willard

I'm Still Praying, Lord!

Sometimes doesn't it seem that if you lined all of your seemingly unanswered prayers end to end, they would surely circle the globe eighty times or more? You pray your fool head off and seek the prayers of hundreds of others. You watch as other women come to faith in Christ, start praying for their husbands, and *boom!* Next thing you know, their husbands are excited and eager to grow in their faith too and lead their families in the Lord. That's when you're tempted to think your prayers are just getting sucked into the air vents in the wall.

I was so sure God would answer this time! Yeah, yeah, I've heard all about somebody's grandma praying for forty years, but I'm tired of waiting. I want results—I want answers!

What you really want is to know that God hasn't forgotten you.

In times of greatest disappointment, one of my greatest comforts comes from the words of the psalmist who wrote, "For the LORD God is a sun and shield; the LORD bestows favor and honor; *no good thing does he withhold from those whose walk is blameless*" (Psalm 84:11, emphasis mine). When it seems as if God is turning a deaf ear toward me and answering everyone else's prayers but mine, I remember the psalmist's words.

First, I remember that, because of my position in Christ, I am counted as blameless. Next, I remind myself that if God will not withhold any good thing from me, then what I've asked for must not be a good thing for me, at least at this time. Then, after my initial disappointment, I'm encouraged. *Thank you, God, for knowing what's good—what's best—for me. Thank you for your sovereignty that says "No," or "Not now." I know that even the best thing—my husband's salvation—is only best when it's in your perfect timing.*

It makes the waiting easier and the disappointments sweeter. And so I keep praying, in hope and in faith, never giving up.

Dear friend, our God hasn't forgotten us, nor will he. He bends his ear and delights in the prayers of his children. He'll use our selfish prayers to change us and our timid, faithless prayers to surprise us when he answers.

So let's get on our knees…and pray.

THINK ON THESE THINGS

- **Think** of some of your past prayers for your unbelieving husband. How has God answered? How have you handled "unanswered" prayer?

- **Study** what the Bible says to us about God's invitation to ask him for what we want. Take note of how we should approach God and what gives us the right to approach him.
  John 1:12-13

Romans 8:15-16
Galatians 4:6-7
Hebrews 4:16
What other scriptures do you find helpful in understanding prayer?

- **Apply** the following scriptures to your understanding of prayer. Since prayer is simply talking to our Father who delights in us, what can we expect?
Psalm 62:8
Luke 11:9-11
1 John 5:14-15
James 5:16

- **Consider** praying Scripture for your husband and your marriage. Take a passage and personalize it. Remember, prayer isn't a magic formula or a means to an end but a way of connecting hearts with the God who loves us.

- "As we pray for our husbands, God gives us the courage to persevere in spite of apparent refusal. As hard as this sometimes seems, it is part of the tribulation or rough way that James says gives our patience a chance to grow (James 1:3). As we pray for our husbands, we come face to face with our own helplessness. We see more and more clearly that we cannot answer our own prayers and therefore must surrender to God's will."

—Beverly Bush Smith and Patricia DeVorss,
Caught in the Middle

What About My Kids?

I'm forever grateful that God has mercy on idiots and fools—and gives grace to the husbands who have to put up with them.

It had only been six or seven months since becoming a Christian when I drew a line in the sand and staked out my No Compromise position where our then-toddler Alison was concerned: *Thou shalt not teach her to believe in Santa Claus.*

In a strategic move in preparation for a counterattack, Barry drew his own line: *Thou art a lunatic—and she's my daughter too. Besides, there's nothing wrong with Santa Claus* and *Jesus at Christmas.*

By the time Laura came along several years later, we'd figured this one out, but back then it escalated into a bloody battle in which neither of us was willing to concede defeat. Anytime Barry would mention Santa Claus, I'd whisk Alison away to "deprogram" her. "Christmas is about Jesus, not Santa Claus," I'd tell her.

Good grief! The child was only two at the time. But in my panic to make sure I raised her "in the nurture and admonition of the Lord," as

I had heard I should, I went overboard. I saw this as a fight for my baby's soul, a spiritual battle in the heavenlies.

Not only that, as far as I was concerned, as the Christian parent, that made me the "better" parent. Therefore, my views were right, which made Barry's wrong. And wrong needed to be conquered with right.

Right?

Wrong. At least regarding my handling of the Santa Claus War. If I had thought it through before I declared "Santa Claus is a tool of the devil, and my child must not come in contact with him or his minions of pointy-eared elves," I would've saved myself a lot of grief.

My husband wasn't forcing Santa worship on our daughter. To his credit, he acknowledged both Santa and Jesus, not one or the other.

I was the inflexible one.

I thought I was doing the right thing before the Lord, but I wasn't. I had reacted out of fear, not out of knowledge, reason, or faith.

As I said, by the time Laura came along, we had decided Santa could stay. After all, he was a historical figure, a man who was said to worship the Christ of Christmas. Barry and I compromised by presenting Santa as "just for fun," like Big Bird or Mickey Mouse. That's all Barry wanted anyway—to have fun with our daughter.

A House Divided

It's true, isn't it? Jesus said he didn't come to bring peace, but a sword (Matthew 10:34). And that sword inflicts such pain, especially when it divides families and pits husband against wife. Especially when it involves the raising of our children. We can handle our own hurts, but when we see our children being caught in the crossfire, the pain causes us to react with fear and with anger. I gave birth to these babies; I WILL see that they get to heaven with me—and no one better stand in my way.

Perhaps the hardest reality is to acknowledge that they're not *my* children, but they're *ours*. Actually, they're God's, but he has given them to both me and my husband to raise together. That means my husband has the same right as I have to say how he would like to raise them. If he wants to put "From Santa" on a gift tag, he has that right. He has that God-given right as head of our family.

But what if he doesn't want our child to attend church? What if he forbids it? What if he believes the Bible is a crock of fairy tales and God is just some mythological figure? What if he's a Hindu and wants to raise our child in his faith? What if he thinks lying is okay and teenage boys should get all the sex they can "as long as they're careful"?

What is a Christian wife supposed to do then?

Can I tell you something? More than knowing the answers to all your what-if questions, you need to know that God knows. He knows your situation, knows your fears, knows the obstacles you face and the turmoil you feel.

It took me more years than it should have to realize that. Before, I used to wrestle with God and question his wisdom and goodness. *Don't you realize that children need a Christian father as a role model? How will daughters know how to choose a Christian man as a husband or sons grow into godly men if they don't know what one is like?*

I have a friend who constantly worries that it would somehow be her fault if her daughters grow up to marry unbelievers. She grieves for the years they never had with a dad who taught them to pray and brought them to church.

But God knows.

I may not ever understand why, but I steadfastly believe that God knew my own daughters needed me as their mother and Barry as their father. They needed—and I needed—our spiritual positions to be exactly as they are. I know this because "my God will meet all [my] needs according to his glorious riches in Christ Jesus" (Philippians

4:19). Also because "the LORD is my shepherd, I shall not be in want" (Psalm 23:1) and "no good thing does he withhold from those whose walk is blameless" (Psalm 84:11). Otherwise, if we had needed a different situation, God who is almighty and sovereign would have provided something different.

Can you see that? Because if you can't, if you haven't reached a point of absolute conviction that God knows exactly what he's doing and is in complete charge and that he is able to do immeasurably more than all we ask or imagine, according to his power that is at work within us, then you won't find rest. Instead, you'll feel out of control as you try to control things in your own strength and wisdom. You'll go off half-cocked and make war over Santa Claus.

That's not to say there won't be times when you'll have to take a stand, and that will come soon enough. For right now, my friend, you need to find security in God's grip. Remember, the Lord knows the plans he has for you, "plans to give you hope and a future," as the prophet Jeremiah wrote (Jeremiah 29:11). You can trust him with yourself, with your children, with your family.

Out of the Mouths of Babes

Like most of my bonehead blunders, it sounded like a good idea at the time. I'd heard all the stories about a child's tender words melting a daddy's heart and moving him to a heartfelt surrendering of himself to Christ. I figured with the right amount of coaching, I could use Alison to get through to her daddy too. Besides, with her brown eyes and dark brown hair—a dead ringer for Barry—I knew he'd be putty in her hands.

So we practiced. "Daddy go church?" "Daddy pray too?"

Since Barry loved the way she said each morning, "Daddy go wook" ("Daddy go work"), I assumed he'd go gaga over this as well.

It took a few tries and the promise of cookies, but Alison performed well. Unfortunately, and despite my feigned surprise, it didn't work like in the stories I'd heard. In fact, I'd say it backfired. Barry caught on right away that I'd turned our daughter into a parrot. Not only had I tried to manipulate him, but I'd used a two-year-old as my puppet.

As I said, it sounded like a good idea at the time. But it's not by might, not by power, not by clever manipulation of a toddler with brown curls, but by God's Spirit that the kingdom is advanced (Zechariah 4:6). God does, indeed, use children to share the gospel with unbelievers, but unless the words are Holy Spirit prompted, they're fruitless.

After years of making just about every mistake imaginable, both with my husband and my kids, I've had lots of time to think. Especially after my plans bomb. I've concluded that most of the mistakes women make in trying to turn their husband's hearts toward the Lord stem from fear, which stems from a lack of faith.

If I'm afraid that God won't work unless I help, I'll enlist my kids to "help" too. Whether intentionally or not, we form an "us against Dad" alliance and either shut him out or conspire against him "because he's not like us." Even if we conspire to influence him with our faith, we're still divided—and I, as mom, am ringleader.

Out of fear, I'm dogmatic and domineering. I try to "protect" my children from the "worldly" influences of their dad and turn him into an enemy. But that's not Christlike, and God is not pleased. *Daddy's a sinner. Mustn't go near him.* Maybe I don't say that in so many words, but my message is clear.

However, my husband is still the one whom God has placed as head of my family for me to love and respect. Part of my job as mom is to teach my children to respect him too. As mom, I set the tone. I set the example. When my kids see me respecting their father, they have a model to follow. And they will follow my model, one way or another. It's up to me to show by my example that respecting the person is different from respecting or condoning the actions.

How do I do this? That's the million-dollar question. The answer is the same as it is with every other aspect of the Christian life: It begins with going to the feet of the Savior.

When Things Get Tough, the Tough Get Praying

Few men want to be bad fathers. From the number of women who bring their kids to church regularly while their husbands stay home, it's safe to say most men are agreeable (or at least tolerant) to their wives raising their children in the faith. Men seem especially agreeable when the children are young. "A little Sunday school never hurt anyone," some may say.

Carolyn's husband, Jack, never misses a Sunday school program their children are involved in; he attends every pancake breakfast, even consents to the kids attending the local Christian school. He just believes Jesus is for women and children.

Margie's husband looks forward to Sunday mornings because that's his time to read the paper, watch the Sunday morning news talk shows, and wash his car. He works hard during the week and wants a day of rest. He's all for his family's religious involvement—just don't try to involve him.

But not every husband is agreeable. Julie says her husband makes her pay one way or another whenever she insists their sons attend church with her. He's cold and makes snide and demeaning remarks to her and about her to the boys. At ages thirteen and fourteen, it's hard enough to get them interested. But with the new youth minister, they've stopped putting up a fight.

Her husband, however, tells the boys, "Jesus will turn you into wimps." He tells Julie they're being brainwashed and offers to take them out fishing and riding motorcycles on Sunday mornings "so they can be real men."

"I'm about ready to give in to him—or kill him," she says. "Or leave. I don't know what to do anymore; it's getting too hard."

At the risk of sounding like a broken record, no matter what the degree of difficulty in your situation, change begins with prayer. As the New Testament writer James tells us, "The prayer of a righteous man is powerful and effective" (James 5:16).

As I said in the previous chapter, prayer is not a sure-fire method of changing situations the way you want them changed. But because the Lord's covenant of grace to us as believers includes our children—and our husbands as well (1 Corinthians 7:14)—he has a vested interest in the spiritual upbringing of our kids and is concerned about what concerns them.

Through prayer, we let our requests be known. *Father, you know how difficult it is! It's not good for the children to see us fighting over faith. Your Word says I'm to raise my children to honor you, but how can I when their dad seems bent on sabotaging my every attempt? I don't even think he's aware of what he's doing or why he's doing it. All I know is it's a battleground, and it's not healthy for any of us. Help! Tell me what to do!*

Because we're his, we have confidence that "if we ask anything according to his will, he hears us. And if we know that he hears us—whatever we ask—we know that we have what we asked of him" (1 John 5:14-15).

Therefore, on behalf of your children, you can pray and ask God to soften your husband's heart and show him the benefits of church attendance or overt evangelism. You can ask that his subversive ploys to draw the children away from the Lord will be thwarted. You can pray about anything regarding the spiritual upbringing of your children. They are part of the covenant—God's covenant with you.

As you pray, your husband's attitudes may change, or you may be strengthened, and God may give you supernatural wisdom to know how to respectfully handle the situation and power to carry it out. It may be instantaneous, or it may take time. Regardless, prayer remains a Christian's greatest weapon against the spiritual forces that would destroy our home life.

Prayer goes before anything else we do.

"Great Will Be Your Children's Peace..."

"When problems in the family are largely over your personal faith that your husband does not share, explain this to the children with tact and sensitivity," writes Michael Fanstone in *Unbelieving Husbands and the Wives Who Love Them.*

A woman named Susan told me that whenever her children ask, "Why doesn't Daddy go to church?" she tells them, "When Daddy's done thinking about everything and decides he can't figure it out, the Holy Spirit will fill in what he needs to know. If we preach at him, he can't listen to the Holy Spirit."

Another woman tells her boys, "God has a plan for our family, and he's not finished yet. It was God's plan that I wouldn't be saved until I was in my twenties and already married and that the two of you would each be saved as little boys. But we don't know God's plan for Dad, so that's why we wait and pray and love him the way he is. And we don't worry."

That's not saying their feelings are always steady or that they don't miss Dad terribly when they go to church without him. But for the most part, she says they've accepted their family situation. "This is the way God wants it right now; if he wanted it different, he would change things. It's that simple," she says.

In the meantime, there are some practical things you can do in raising your kids in the Lord. Several years ago in a *Christian Parenting Today* article entitled "Reconcilable Differences," marriage counselors Les and Leslie Parrott advised the Christian parent in a spiritually unequal home to find common ground when it comes to the values you want your children to embrace. Biblical principles are universal; they're practical as well as spiritual, such as "Don't lie" and "Don't steal." Most likely the values found in the Bible are the same values your husband wants your children to live by as well.

"So while your partner may not join you in offering godly explanations, you can take advantage of countless one-on-one opportunities to teach your children godly ways," write the Parrotts. "This isn't a technique for going behind your partner's back; it's a way of living out your convictions. It's a way of being you."

As Christians, we're always to be ready to give an answer when asked about our faith, and children are always asking questions. Moses, in the book of Deuteronomy goes further and instructs believers to take the commandments of God and impress them upon our children "when you sit at home and when you walk along the road, when you lie down and when you get up" (Deuteronomy 6:7).

Let's not forget the witness of our lives. It's been said that values are more often "caught" than "taught," and actions do speak louder than words. So even if one parent adamantly opposes the Christian faith, our children will see our responses to life's challenges, whether they're faith-filled or faith-less. Either way, they'll learn by our example what it means to be in Christ.

Also, never underestimate the power of the Holy Spirit to speak to a child's heart. Pray and ask the Spirit to be your children's teacher—and then trust him to answer your request. Part of his role is to convict people of their sin and to lead them into "all truth." And because our children are part of God's covenant with us, we can be confident that he will enable and empower us to pass down our heritage of faith to them.

Want some good news? Through our union with Christ, we've begun a new spiritual generation. God's punishment passes down to three and four generations of those who disobey him, but he shows love to a thousand generations to those he calls his own (Deuteronomy 5:9-10). That's me and you and our children and our grandchildren—and their great-great-great-grandchildren!

Tell me that's not encouraging.

Even so, it's not without struggle. The bottom line is, we are to obey God rather than men (Acts 5:29), and God charges us with the responsibility of raising our children to honor him. However, he doesn't leave us helpless or defenseless. Instead, he equips us with everything we need to carry out his commands—even when we think all is hopeless and that the obstacles are too great. That's often when he surprises us in the process, as a woman named Diana discovered. After years of making her Sunday mornings nearly unbearable as she tried to get their sons ready for church, one morning her husband got up out of bed and quietly went out to the garage and warmed up the car.

That's all he did. He didn't go to church with them, but Diana says that was a giant step. "Just when you think all is hopeless, it isn't," she told me. "God's encouragement comes exactly when you need it most. Sometimes it's the little things that speak the loudest to your heart."

She said that small gesture set a whole new tone for her and her boys on the ride to church. Her hope was renewed that God was, indeed, doing something in the life of her family. She said as they drove to church, they all thanked God for Daddy. "That's what I think my boys need most, at least right now."

Louise says, "Even though my girls are grown, I often look back and wonder what their lives would be like if we had all had the same spiritual focus, if we all had loved Jesus together. But I'm a realist. What's past is past, and no amount of wishing and wondering can change a thing. Besides, God has faithfully kept all his promises and has given me sufficient grace to teach my girls his ways."

As the prophet Isaiah wrote, "All your sons will be taught by the LORD, and great will be your children's peace" (Isaiah 54:13). We can cling to this promise as he shows himself to be a Father, a Teacher, a Comforter, a Friend to our children and also to us. As for me, I have no doubt whatsoever that God designed my family exactly the way it is. Knowing that it comes from the hand of my loving, gracious Father is sufficiently, hopefully, gracefully, thankfully...enough.

THINK ON THESE THINGS

- **Think** about holding a baby in your arms. What kinds of things do you want to teach this child? If you have children, how have you been able to pass on your faith to them—even if you're their only Christian parent?

- **Study** the instructions God gives to Christian parents:
  Deuteronomy 6:4-9
  Proverbs 22:15
  Proverbs 23:13
  Proverbs 29:15
  Proverbs 30:17
  Even with a husband who is hostile toward overt Christian teaching, it is possible to still pass on your faith. What encouragement do the following scriptures give?

Isaiah 49:25

Isaiah 54:11-13

1 Corinthians 7:14

- **Apply** the following scriptures to a spiritually unequal family. What do you learn about God's intervention and help in difficult situations?
  Exodus 2:1-10
  1 Samuel 3
  Psalm 103:17-18
  Matthew 2

- **Consider** the instruction from God to the children of Israel in Joshua 4 to set up "monuments," or physical signs or symbols that have spiritual significance. As you see God's hand in the lives of your children, put a stone or something of significance into a box or jar. When your children ask about the stones, tell them what God has done. Use them for your own remembrance as well.

- "Do you ever feel responsible for your partner's lack of faith—that somehow, some way, if you could just do or be something different, your spouse would become a Christian? Don't pummel yourself with guilt feelings. Self-punishment will do nothing but undermine your capacity to be who you really are—a child of God, freely forgiven. Truth be known, if you don't recognize and resolve your feelings of guilt, and if you don't rely on God's grace, you'll end up projecting feelings of guilt onto your children and your partner. Nothing could be worse, for guilt cuts the heart out of a healthy home."

  —Les and Leslie Parrott, "Reconcilable Differences"
  (*Christian Parenting Today*, 1995)

What Should I
Do About...?

*I*t's Friday night. Your husband comes home in a great mood. He tells
you to change your clothes—he's discovered a little bar over on the
other side of town that plays '80s rock, and he wants you to go with
him. What do you do?

The phone rings. Just as you go to pick it up, your husband calls
from the couch, "If that's for me, tell them I'm not home." It's for him.
What do you do?

Your husband calls home and starts to tell you a joke he's just heard.
Halfway into it you realize it's dirty. Not only that, it's *funny*. Do you
laugh? What do you do?

You go out to the trash can and count eight beer bottles. You find a
stash of pot or a porn video in the back of a closet. What do you do?

Sometimes they're just sticky wickets. Those touchy, questionable
situations that you simply don't know how to handle. Sometimes, however, you know what to do, but doing it is certain to cause even more

problems than you already have. And sometimes the situation you face is potentially devastating to you, your husband, your marriage, your family.

What do you do?

Wouldn't it be great to have a handbook that has specific answers to every conceivable situation that could arise? *When your husband does or says A, turn to page 73 and follow steps 1-4, and this will be the result.*

But life isn't like that. Not every situation has a tidy answer and a guaranteed outcome. That's where a deep knowledge of the Word of God comes in. The psalmist wrote, "Your word is a lamp to my feet and a light for my path" (Psalm 119:105) and "I have hidden your word in my heart that I might not sin against you" (Psalm 119:11).

When we know the Word of God and are familiar enough with its basic principles, then knowing what to do when confronted with sticky wickets and tough situations becomes easier. Of course, knowing what to do based on Scripture and actually doing it are two different subjects. That's where stepping out in faith comes in.

Shades of Gray

Donna confides, "My husband is always telling me dirty jokes. I know he's not being malicious, and some of them really are funny, and I can't help laughing. But then I feel like I'm a 'bad witness.' What should I do?"

Good question. As I see it, she has two options: She could frown disapprovingly, shake her finger at her husband, and try to shame him for such despicable behavior. She could quote Scripture about not letting any unwholesome talk come out of his mouth (Ephesians 4:29) and how on the Day of Judgment he'll have to give an account for every careless word spoken (Matthew 12:36). She could call him a disgusting pig.

Or she could speak to him from her heart. "Honey, to me, sex with you is so precious that jokes like that demean what we share together as lovers." That way she gets her message across ("I don't like dirty jokes") without making him feel like he's being scolded. She upholds a biblical principle—sex is a gift to be enjoyed by a husband and wife—without having to mention "Thus saith the Lord." Depending on her husband's openness to spiritual truth, this could lead into a great discussion about an area that men are already interested in.

Will it work? Only God knows. What it will do is convey her feelings with grace and respect. The results are between God and her husband. The bottom line: No one can change a person's heart, and a Christian wife cannot and should not expect her unbelieving husband to exhibit Christian behavior. To try and persuade, even force, him to "behave Christianly" is to present him with a wrong gospel. However, we have every right to voice our opinions and convey our feelings.

A similar area of potential conflict is the use of bad language. Some people use it without thinking, and it's everywhere. Again, a wife could turn this into a major source of contention and conflict and attempt to force her husband into compliance by scolding or shaming. But that rarely works.

It could well be that there's nothing you can do or say to change your husband's choice of words. You can tell him once or twice that you would appreciate his not swearing in your presence and especially not in front of the children. When it comes to misusing the Lord's name, tell him that it particularly hurts you. But after that, it's best to drop it. Nagging never changed anyone's heart except to make it harder.

Years ago I learned a successful method of communication that has stuck with me. When attempting to get your feelings across to someone, use comparison. For example, if I want Barry to know exactly how much something bothers me, I might say to him, "You know how much you hate it when people point their fingers at you?" As soon as I say that, his eyes narrow and his fists clench. He *hates* finger pointing.

If his language was a problem, I might say, "As much as you hate finger pointing, that's how much I hate hearing you swear." That way, I've shared my feelings in a way he understands. Again, whether or not he does anything about it is no longer my concern.

My concern, even before I say anything, is to make it a focus for prayer. *Lord, help me to demonstrate in love how his words can both help or hurt me and those around him so that he will be aware of the power of his words. Help him to see, to hear, to understand. Open his eyes to know that what comes out of his mouth is what's in his heart. Help me, Lord, to be loving and respectful toward him, regardless of his behavior, as I trust in you to put my emotions at rest.*

Another gray area is leisure activities, how you and your husband spend your time together. I know how hard it is to find a decent movie to go to or video to rent. And there's nothing wrong with voicing your opinion. ("I'd rather not see people getting hacked to death or watch other people having sex.") However, before you open your mouth, check yourself for a self-righteous or judgmental attitude. Ask the Lord to give you a humble heart and the right words to say, and trust him that he will.

What about other activities? What if your husband likes to go to bars or parties where there's a lot of drinking and you've decided, as a Christian, you don't want to drink? Should you refuse to go and stay home? Insist your husband do so too? It's a sticky wicket, isn't it?

On the one hand, the closer our walk with the Lord, the less appealing hanging out in a bar sounds. On the other, the Lord has placed us with this particular husband to be a light in the darkness—in his darkness.

Biblically, we have no law prohibiting us from attending a party or going to a bar with our husbands. We have every biblical right even to drink alcohol with a clear conscience. "Everything is permissible," Paul tells the Corinthian believers, "but not everything is beneficial" (1 Corinthians 10:23). He goes on to say we shouldn't seek our own good, but the good of others, and then tells believers to go ahead and "eat anything sold in the meat market without raising questions of conscience" (verse 25). If an unbeliever invites you to a meal and you want to go—go and enjoy the meal.

While Paul was specifically addressing what a believer should do when eating meat that had been sacrificed to idols by a dinner host, we can apply the same principle when it comes to going out with our husbands: "Whatever you do, do it all for the glory of God" (verse 31). If your intention is to be your husband's companion and the Lord's light in the darkness, and if it does not violate any civil law or any of God's commands, then you can do so with a clear conscience.

BUT if parties and bars are a problem and a temptation for you, for example, if you've had an alcohol problem in the past, then by all means, *don't go*. Tell your husband, "I've decided I no longer want to drink, and going to a bar would be too much of a temptation for me." Then suggest something else for the two of you to do together. This conveys an "I" message ("I have a problem"), while letting him know you still want to be with him ("Let's go play miniature golf—I'll even let you win this time").

What if your husband wants to go anyway? It may mean you stay home alone. Nobody said the Christian life was easy. But above all, especially if you're recovering from your own alcohol abuse, you need to guard your own heart and keep yourself from temptation.

No matter what situation arises, ask God for wisdom. He promises to give it generously to all who ask (James 1:5). We don't always know what to do, but we can be confident that he does.

Between a Rock and a Hard Place

I have a friend whose husband professes to be a Christian. Even so, every time the phone rings he tells her, "Whoever it is, I'm not home."

While it's comforting (in a disturbing sort of way) to know that dealing with hard situations isn't exclusive to the spiritually unequal marriage, that doesn't make it easy when faced with a decision to make.

Actually, choosing whether or not to lie for someone is a whole lot easier than choosing a suitable movie to watch. God clearly tells us not to lie. When the choice comes down to obeying God or pleasing your husband, we must obey God regardless of the outcome.

In my friend's case, she plainly tells her husband, "I'm not going to lie for you." She has set a standard and refuses to move from it. Of course, her husband doesn't like it, but that's his problem. A practical way around this particular situation might be to let the answering machine pick up all their calls, although that doesn't deal with the heart issues. For example, what if the lying involves signing a dishonest income tax return? There isn't a mechanical way around that. That's why a person needs to determine ahead of time which moral issues are nonnegotiable, using the Bible as the standard.

Simply put, if God clearly or implicitly says no, then don't do it. Likewise, if he says to do something, then that's what you need to do, trusting him to always give enough grace, strength, and power to do the right thing, despite any opposition.

When I was a new Christian and started attending a local church, I wanted to put money in the offering plate. However, for the first time in my life since age thirteen, I didn't have a job or any source of my own income. Also, our finances at the time were tight. I went to my church and asked the advice of a godly older woman who told me not to take any of our household money to use as an offering without Barry's approval.

However, I still wanted to give the Lord an offering for Christmas, which was three months away. So I prayed. I told God I didn't have any money of my own, but if I happened to receive any money in my name by my birthday (December 10), I wanted to give it to Jesus as his birthday gift.

I shouldn't have been surprised, but money started pouring in from everywhere. It was wild! On the morning of December 10, I had $50. I also had a stack of bills on the kitchen table, and Barry suggested I use the money to pay one or two of them.

"But I promised I'd give this money to Jesus," I told him, then added, "I don't know how, but I know God will bless us if we give it to him."

That was too much for Barry to take. He had been working twelve-hour days to support us—and I wanted to give money away! At that, he said he wanted a divorce, then left for work.

Stunned at his announcement, I immediately grabbed the phone to call my friend Terry to commiserate. As I started whining, I began opening the morning mail that came while I was on the phone. I opened one envelope after another—all addressed to me—all containing money. By the time I was through, I had $150!

Barry came in from work later that day, absolutely shocked to find me grinning and dancing around. After all, *on my birthday* he had said he wanted a divorce. Unable to contain my excitement, I showed him the money and said, "Look, Barry, I told you God would bless us!"

I'll never forget his face. It clearly said, "Well, what do you know? God really did bless!" He apologized for the divorce remark, and together we agreed to use the original $50 to give anonymously to a family in need from the church. Then we used the rest to pay bills. After that, giving to the church has never been an issue between us, but I always let Barry set the amount.

I tell you this story because I know that money issues can destroy a marriage. But I also know that God has creative solutions to any conflict the two of you may have, even money matters and giving to the church.

Another hard area is church attendance when your husband "forbids" it. I'm sure you've heard all the opinions, from "submit to your husband in all things, including this, and he will be won by your behavior," to "you tell that man he doesn't own you, and you'll go to church if you want to—and you don't care what he says." Although I like the sassiness of the second opinion, they are both only opinions. Our standard for everything must always be, "What does the Bible say?"

In the area of church attendance, it says, "Let us not give up meeting together, as some are in the habit of doing" (Hebrews 10:25). That verse is preceded by a call to persevere and to hold on to the hope we profess, a reminder of God's faithfulness and an urging to spur one another on toward love and good deeds.

We need to meet together regularly with like-minded believers or else we won't persevere; we'll lose our hope and forget about God's faithfulness. We'll fall away and forget about the grace of God.

I met a woman at a dinner one night. As we started talking about this book I had just started writing, she said, "Oh, I could fill all your pages with my life!" She had just divorced her husband, an unbeliever, which wasn't the type of testimony I was looking for. However, she did have one thing to say that I found exceptionally profound. When I asked her, "What was the worst piece of advice you ever received concerning your unequal marriage?" she didn't hesitate to answer.

She told me, "When my husband was giving me all kinds of grief about going to church, my pastor told me, 'Then stop going. God will understand.' I can tell you, things went downhill fast after that because I fell away."

Another woman, whose still-unbelieving husband has started attending church, said her husband gave her a hard time too in the beginning, but she remained steadfast in her commitment to do the things she knew God required her to do. It wasn't easy either, but she said she thought about all the Christians around the world who were persecuted and even killed for their faith. Snide remarks from her husband were nothing in comparison to what some suffered.

After she had been a Christian for about a year, she overheard her husband's end of a phone conversation with her own (also unbelieving) mother. He said, "I thought she'd give this Jesus thing up, but she hasn't—I think it's real."

A few months later, when he started going to church with her, he commented, "You never backed down." His harassment of her was his way of testing the reality of her belief and the genuineness of her commitment. It was worth taking a stand, she said.

Does this mean a woman should dogmatically attend every church service offered? I believe wives in an unequally yoked marriage walk a tightrope. Although a Christian's highest allegiance is to God, wives are still called to submit to their husbands. The good news is, God is a God of grace. He won't smite any of his children with brimstone for missing an occasional service, but as a rule, we should "not give up meeting together, as some are in the habit of doing," no matter how difficult it may be.

In most instances, occasional compromise isn't necessarily bad: *Sunday mornings I go to church; the rest of the day I'll spend with you.* You may have to bypass Sunday and Wednesday night services if it involves too much conflict. Even if it doesn't, too much time "at that place," as Lynn's husband calls it, often breeds resentment.

Another option might be attending a women's Bible study while your husband is at work. Ask God to lead you into creative outlets for study, fellowship, and worship. Remember, he desires that for you more than you desire it for yourself.

When it comes to handling any hard situation, when obeying God means having to face hostility, anger, ridicule, threats, etc., we have the assurance of knowing we are under no obligation to submit to our husbands' demands to do anything that violates God's law. We also have the assurance that God's grace will always be sufficient for everything the Lord requires us to do.

In the gospel of John, many of the disciples turned away after things started to get tough. Jesus asked the Twelve if they wanted to leave too. Peter answered, "Lord, to whom shall we go? You have the words of eternal life" (John 6:68). When things get tough, when you feel as if you're between a rock and a hard place, turn to the Rock. He alone has the words of eternal life.

To whom else would you go?

Nothing Is Impossible with God, Not Even _____

An e-mail from a friend says it all: "I'm just so sick of his drinking, I'm about to explode! He says such horrible things about me in front of the kids. What am I supposed to do?"

Another woman, a fairly new Christian, says, "He's *always* drinking. I just keep praying he'll grow up. Meanwhile, I can only go one day at a time because I never know what he'll be like. The scariest part: There's a guy at work who's been flattering me. Then I have to go home to... Well, it's definitely hard."

Yet another woman has been living with her pot-smoking husband for forty years (although she says for the first twenty he was "just a drunkard"). For the past twenty years, not only has he smoked marijuana, but he's been growing it as well.

If you have ears to hear, the stories are endless. Although the majority of the women I talked with concerning their spiritually unequal marriages describe their husbands as "good-hearted" and generally not excessively antagonistic about matters of faith, there are quite a few who categorize themselves in what one woman called a "perpetual battle zone."

Of these women who admit to being in these battle-zone situations, most deal with a husband's addiction: alcohol, illegal drugs, and pornography. In addition to the spiritual conflict that comes with being in a spiritually mismatched marriage, these women contend with an added dimension.

Friend, if you're one of these hurting wives, my heart goes out to you. As I write this, I'm praying that the Lord will pour out an extra blessing on your life this day. I may not know the degree of your hardship, but I do know that nothing is impossible with God. Please don't isolate yourself in your situation, but seek help. Check your telephone book or call a local church for a referral for a Bible-based, Christian support group to help you handle addiction-related problems.

"Don't be alone in your situation, and learn to lovingly confront," advises Brenda Waggoner, a licensed professional counselor in Texas as well as the author of *The Velveteen Woman.* "While we as Christian wives are to have a gentle and quiet spirit, too often we think that means we sit back and 'just pray.' But that doesn't bring about change and it fails to hold a husband accountable."

She adds, before you do anything to confront your particular situation, make sure you're willing to do whatever it takes to facilitate change. Count the cost, but do the right thing—and for the right reason.

Waggoner says your attitude needs to be: "I love you. I want our marriage to work out, but the things that are going on are not healthy for either one of us."

Next, seek counseling. Ideally, both you and your husband should go. A nonthreatening way to approach your husband is to say, "Because I love you and am committed to our marriage, I'm going to seek counseling. Are you interested in going with me?" If your husband refuses, go without him. You need help as much as he does, even if it's just someone objective to talk to.

Waggoner says a common heartache affecting many marriages, even marriages where both spouses are Christians, is pornography. "For the woman whose husband has this particular problem, it feels the same as if he were having an affair," she says. "It diminishes her sense of self-worth; she feels disrespected by her husband. It also greatly affects the quality of their sexual life because the woman feels like she's being used."

To women who are dealing with this, she urges them to see a counselor. For the women she sees in her practice, she often offers the following advice:

- Confront your husband with the truth of your feelings and communicate your hurt. "To me, it feels as if you're with another woman when you're (watching that movie, looking at that Web site). That hurts, especially when you're finished and you want to have sex with me. I feel it's not me you love, but you're just using me." Waggoner says sometimes men will respond to that message. To them, the pornography is just a picture on a screen or a page, and they don't realize their wives see it as an emotional issue.

- When your husband finishes viewing pornography and approaches you for sex, make a tough stand for truthfulness by saying, "I can't respond to you right now; I'm too hurt." Attitude is key, says Waggoner, and as with any type of confrontation, this needs to be surrounded with prayer. The goal is allowing your husband to face his sin and his need for help. Therefore, your motivation should never be anger, retaliation, or punishment.

- If the pornography use continues, the next step is an "in-house" separation—separate bedrooms. Waggoner says this works well in getting a man's attention.

In all these areas, keep in mind that your husband has a problem, but he is not the problem itself. As with everything, your mind-set needs to be "This is my husband, and I'll do whatever it takes to help him." (For abuse situations, see chapter 13.)

A woman married to a longtime drug user says, "The Lord allowed this situation to happen and I will trust him to do whatever he needs to do in and through me." She knows there are no guarantees that her husband will ever change. The only guarantee she—we—have is that nothing is impossible with God...and that nothing, neither life nor death nor anything the world throws at us, will ever separate us from the love of God for us in Christ Jesus.

And if God is for us, who or what could ever possibly be against us?

THINK ON THESE THINGS

- **Think** about some common areas of conflict wives of unbelieving husbands face. Which ones violate Scripture and which merely violate personal taste or culture?

- **Study** what God's Word says about seeking solutions to these dilemmas and about what our attitude should be.
  Galatians 6:1
  Ephesians 4:15
  Philippians 4:6-7
  Colossians 1:9-14
  Go back and study the life of Joseph, especially regarding his encounter with Potiphar's wife (Genesis 39). What stand did he take with her?

- **Apply** God's armor daily (found in Ephesians 6:10-18). God has given us his armor as protection against the bombardment of ungodly influences. As you apply each element listed in the passage, meditate on how it protects you in the battle. (Remember: You're not battling your husband, but unseen forces that wreak havoc in your life.)

- **Consider** the promises found in the Bible. When circumstances seem insurmountable, what is our hope? Keep a small notebook of Bible promises that you find especially helpful. Here's one to get you started: "And God is able to make all grace abound to you, so that in all things at all times, having all that you need, you will abound in every good work" (2 Corinthians 9:8).

- "There isn't always a pain-free way to tell the truth, but the alternative is a marriage built around a series of covert compromises. Truth may initially douse the fires of passion, but over time it creates new possibilities for genuine intimacy—the intimacy that comes with being fully known by another."

  —David L. Goetz, *Couples Devotional Bible*

Thirteen

Is It Ever Okay
to Leave?

S he had short curly hair and a bunch of kids. I only talked with her
briefly while visiting a "moms without partners" Sunday school
class at a nearby church.

"I struggled with the decision to divorce," she said, "because I know
tearing my marriage apart is sin."

She went on to explain that she had become a Christian after she
married her husband, but because of her in-laws' involvement in a non-
Christian religion and their overbearing influence on her and her children, she stayed away from any church at all and fell away from her own
faith.

Then life at home became difficult. Her husband's drinking
increased; so did his verbal and emotional abuse. That drove her back to
the Cross where she renewed her commitment to Christ, was baptized—
then filed for divorce.

"I knew that was wrong, but I still did it," she said. "Even after the divorce, I tried to get my husband to go with me to see the pastor for counseling to get our marriage back together, but he doesn't want to change."

And so this mother of five is left with the effects of her divorce on her family.

A man named Frank recently sent me a copy of his testimony. He had grown up watching his alcoholic, unbelieving father routinely beat his Christian mother. She refused to leave, trusting instead that one day her husband would come to faith in Christ and change if only she were submissive enough.

His father eventually did—and Frank said it was through witnessing his mother's endurance of her sufferings that he himself became a Christian—but it was not without some damage being done. Frank admitted that before he came to Christ, he followed his father's example as an alcoholic and an abuser. He wonders if his mother should have left his father and taken him with her while he was young.

Candace says she knows too well why God says he *hates* divorce. She stuck with her unbelieving husband through twelve years of his alcoholism and drug use and his on-again, off-again rehab programs. She prayed nonstop for him, sought counseling for herself, and surrounded herself with Christian friends.

Although her marriage was difficult, she never lost hope. She believed God. She believed—still believes—marriage is forever. What God had joined together, no man could tear apart.

Then her husband told her about his girlfriend, and Candace's world fell apart.

"Even then I didn't want to pursue a divorce," she told me. "I still believe God hates divorce and that we could get through it. I trusted that if I prayed enough and waited, that God would change Tim's heart—that he'd use this to show Tim his need for Jesus."

Candace's faith remained firm. Tim moved the family to another state to start fresh, but they were there only one week before he returned to his girlfriend.

Candace was devastated but still didn't pursue a divorce. However, after two years of Tim's vacillating between his family and his girlfriend, he filed for divorce. Now that my friend is finally recovering from the whole ordeal—faith firmly intact—her only question is: Can she, as a Christian, ever remarry?

What God Has Joined Together...

Life doesn't make sense. I've been thinking a lot lately about why some marriages survive and why many, even Christian marriages, don't. I guess it boils down to sinful people: Where they're involved, there are no guarantees. And yes, God can and often does intervene, but sometimes he lets sinful people go their own way.

Still...*God hates divorce.* As the prophet Malachi writes, "Has not the LORD made them one? In flesh and spirit they are his. And why one? Because he was seeking godly offspring. So guard yourself in your spirit, and do not break faith with the wife of your youth. 'I hate divorce,' says the LORD God of Israel" (Malachi 2:15-16).

Even from the beginning, way back in the Garden of Eden, God's purpose for marriage has always been one man, one woman, one flesh until death.

When challenged on this, Jesus told those who were looking for loopholes, "What God has joined together, let man not separate" (Matthew 19:6). That's the ideal. That's God's best. That's what we're to pursue and work toward, hope for, pray for. But because of the "hardness of people's hearts," as Jesus described it, the Law of Moses permitted divorce for reasons of adultery.

The apostle Paul, addressing believing spouses, further instructed them not to divorce an unbelieving spouse just because he or she wasn't a Christian. No such thing as "irreconcilable differences." However, if an unbeliever leaves, "let him do so. A believing man or woman is not bound in such circumstances" (1 Corinthians 7:15).

So from a biblical perspective, only adultery and desertion are grounds for divorce. That's not saying a Christian *must* pursue divorce for these reasons, only that one may. Working things out is always the best-case scenario, especially when children are involved.

When Love Turns Angry

The American Medical Association has declared domestic violence against women a "national epidemic." Statistics from the Bureau of Justice show a woman is beaten every fifteen seconds. Domestic violence is the leading cause of injury to women between the ages of fifteen and forty-four—that's more than car accidents, muggings, and rapes combined.

A national survey of more than six thousand families revealed that 50 percent of the men who frequently assaulted their wives also abused their children. Also, men who have witnessed their parents' domestic violence are three times more likely to abuse their own wives than men with nonviolent parents.

Such sad statistics. I can't even comprehend what a woman in an abusive situation has to contend with every day, and I'm tempted to skip over this subject altogether. But because the odds are that you or someone you know will be affected in some way by abuse, I can't ignore it. And a spiritually unequal marriage often adds fuel to an already volatile situation.

"Abuse crushes a woman's spirit," says licensed counselor Brenda Waggoner. "It doesn't help to allow yourself to be abused, whether verbally, emotionally, or physically." She says she counsels many women who feel trapped and hopeless in their situations.

Waggoner says *any* abuse needs to be faced and dealt with. Not doing anything, being a submissive doormat and accepting abuse, doesn't help anyone. The woman allows herself to be diminished as a person; the children are subjected to turmoil and chaos, not to mention they learn to be abusers themselves; and doing nothing fails to hold the abuser accountable and only encourages the abuse to continue.

"He's controlling her, and as long as that works, he'll continue," Waggoner says. "What usually happens is the man places blame on the woman—'It's your fault.' But he's only avoiding his own issues."

When the abuse is limited to a husband's verbal outbursts and tirades, she says a woman can often calmly, but firmly, put things back on him. She says one of the best ways to handle a verbal abuser is to tell him, "If you decide to keep doing this, I'm going to have to leave until you cool off." This is a nonintrusive way of getting his attention. If he doesn't have an audience, if he sees that his outbursts aren't working and the benefits he gets out of his controlling behavior are taken away, the hope is that he'll get the message and stop, or at least recognize that he needs help.

Friend, if you are in a marriage where there is any kind of abuse—verbal, emotional, and especially physical—seek professional help. In his book *Counseling Insights,* Chuck Swindoll tells pastors and other counselors that it's "unrealistic and unfair to think that regardless of sure danger and possible loss of life, a godly mate and helpless children should subject themselves to brutality and other forms of extreme treatment. At that point, commitment to Christ supersedes all other principles in a home."

He goes on to say he doesn't advocate divorce but rather restraint and safety through separation. "It's one thing to be in subjection. It is another thing entirely to become the brunt of indignity, physical assault, sexual perversion, and uncontrolled rage. Since the believer's body is the temple of God's Spirit, it is *unthinkable* that he is pleased to have our bodies mauled and mistreated by sick and/or thoughtless mates who care little about their family's welfare and think of nothing but their own twisted gratification."

When love turns angry, and you're being crushed and diminished, cry out for help—immediately. Trust that God, who is your Protector and Guide, will direct you to the right people. First go to your own church and inform them of your situation. If you don't have one, or if they can't (or sadly, won't) respond to you in a timely or compassionate manner, go to another church or Christian care organization in your area. Flee to an abuse shelter if you can—and pray, pray, *pray*. Ask God for safety, provision, and sufficient grace. Ask him to calm your spirit, clear your mind, sort out your thoughts and emotions. Ask the Lord for wisdom and strength. And pray for your husband.

In the Old Testament book of Genesis, Abraham's wife, Sarah, had a maidservant named Hagar. Twice Hagar suffered mistreatment at the hands of her owners: once when she became pregnant by Abraham—at Sarah's suggestion—and then again after Hagar's son was born. Each time she was banished into the desert; each time she broke down weeping. Each time God appeared to her and revealed himself as "the God who sees." He saw her mistreatment and came to her defense.

Take heart, friend. God sees everything you suffer and has made an unbreakable covenant with you to be on your side and to contend with those who contend with you.

I can't promise your road will be easy or without obstacles. Leaving an abusive situation might be equally as difficult as staying. But I do know that the Lord knows the plans he has for you, "plans to prosper you and not to harm you, plans to give you hope and a future" (Jeremiah 29:11).

Not only that, listen to what the Lord says after that: "'Then you will call upon me and come and pray to me, and I will listen to you. You will seek me and find me when you seek me with all your heart. I will be found by you,' declares the LORD, *'and will bring you back from captivity'*" (Jeremiah 29:12-14, emphasis mine).

Again, take heart. As the psalmist wrote, "Weeping may endure for a night, but joy comes in the morning" (Psalm 30:5, NKJV).

When There's Someone Else

As a new Christian, Emily was distraught. Her unbelieving husband had come home and, filled with remorse, confessed that he'd had sex with another woman. It was a one-time thing, just someone he'd met in a bar. He swore he'd never do it again.

After the initial shock of his confession wore off, she said she was filled with such pity for him and a strange sense of forgiveness and compassion that she could only attribute it to God's Spirit in her life.

But not fully understanding the Scriptures, she thought she was *required* to seek a divorce from her husband because of his infidelity. That's why she was so distraught.

In an e-mail she wrote, "I thank God that I had a wise Christian friend to help me through this. It's not okay that my husband did that—he'll have to deal with his own guilt and consequences, and I'm praying that God will use this to help him see his need for a Savior. But I know it was only that one time and not a pattern. Sure it hurt and I let him know I was hurt, but I also see this as an opportunity to let him see the supernatural forgiveness that only Christians can give."

I got another e-mail from a woman, also married to an unbeliever, whose husband started an affair with a coworker. After discussing it with her pastor, she decided not to do anything impulsive.

As she prayed daily, even hourly, for God to show her what to do, her husband continued his adulterous behavior. She said that she remained silent and continued her regular activities of going to church, keeping the house, and taking care of their two small sons. At one point her husband suggested they divorce, but he never followed through.

"Over time the affair fizzled, and he decided to stay," she wrote. "My life was bathed in much fervent prayer. Then out of the blue he started coming to church with me. He eventually professed Christ, was baptized, and, in his words, started over. He's now a deacon and a teacher in our church. It's been eighteen years since the problems. God is good. Sometimes all you can do is hold on to his promises."

Sometimes, as Ralph Waldo Emerson observed, "the only way out is through." Hang on tight, pray with all your might, and wait until you come out on the other side. But when it comes to adultery, sometimes you can't hang on tight. Sometimes there is no other side—the affair doesn't fizzle, or your husband finds yet another woman. God takes such behavior seriously enough to say that's the one thing that breaks a marriage bond. It's that devastating.

Even so, divorce should be a last resort. "Why then…did Moses *command* that a man give his wife a certificate of divorce and send her away?" some Pharisees asked Jesus.

Setting them straight, Jesus told them, "Moses *permitted* you to divorce your wives because your hearts were hard" (Matthew 19:7-8, emphasis mine). When it comes to hard hearts and adultery, love must be tough, according to James Dobson in his book of the same title. Contrary to counsel sometimes offered to women with cheating husbands, permissive, unconditional acceptance of a husband's infidelity is *not* the loving, Christian thing to do.

"Genuine love *demands* toughness in moments of crisis," Dobson writes. "What they need in that moment is loving discipline that forces them to choose between good and bad alternatives. What they don't need…is permissiveness, understanding, excuses, removal of guilt, and buckets of tender loving care. To dole out that kind of smother-love at such a time [as continued adulterous behavior] is to reinforce irresponsibility and generate disrespect. It deprives the marriage of *mutual accountability!*"

When a Christian wife is confronted with her husband's adultery, her first line of offense, as with everything, is with prayer. Then she needs to seek professional Christian counseling. With the help of a counselor, she needs to confront her husband and, as Dobson recommends, force a crisis, especially with a man who's "torn between two lovers."

For the man who can't decide who he wants to be with, his wife or someone else, Dobson says the most loving thing a woman can do is present him with a choice, with the consequences clearly spelled out: *If you continue with this behavior, you stand to lose everything of value to you—your home, your children, your wife, your reputation.* It's his choice.

"The choice will rest with the unfaithful partner," he writes. "But it must be clear to him that he cannot have it both ways…in fact, the best thing that can happen to a tomcat who prowls around at night is to come home after his first escapade to face reality. Right then, in the aftermath of his foolishness, he needs to feel the full impact of his sin."

You, as the Christian wife, must always keep the door open for genuine repentance and reconciliation while standing firm in not enabling or indulging your husband's adultery. Remember, you can do all things through Christ who gives you strength (Philippians 4:13).

While taking a tough stand doesn't guarantee a husband will quit his fooling around or a confrontation will bring him to faith in Christ, it's the best thing a woman can do—for her husband and for herself.

And if a husband chooses to leave? As painful as that may be, if that happens, a Christian is free to let him leave. The marriage covenant is broken, and the woman is free to remarry another Christian.

Friend, if any of these situations apply to you, know that you're not alone or without help or hope. Keep praying; keep seeking godly counsel. Don't go through any of this alone. Even if you're feeling worthless and your spirit is broken, keep in mind that God sees you. He hears your cries. He knows your pain...and he's able:

"To make all grace abound to you."
(2 Corinthians 9:8)
"To deal gently with those who are ignorant and are going astray."
(Hebrews 5:2)
"To keep you from falling and to present you
before his glorious presence without fault and with great joy."
(Jude 24)
"To do immeasurably more than all we ask or imagine,
according to his power that is at work within us."
(Ephesians 3:20)
Amen.

THINK ON THESE THINGS

- **Think** about the result divorce has had on our culture, even in your own community or family. The Bible is clear: God hates divorce. How many people do you know who have been affected by divorce?

- **Study** the following passages that discuss divorce.
  Malachi 2:13-16
  Matthew 5:31-32; 19:3-11
  1 Corinthians 7:1-16
  What are the only reasons God gives for divorce? Why do you think that is?

- **Apply** these scriptures to your own life if you've entertained thoughts of divorce. What are some other options? (Note: If you are divorced and remarried, be encouraged that you are forgiven in Christ—no condemnation!)

- **Consider** steps to take if you're involved in an abusive situation. From *Dangerous Marriage* by S. R. and Linda McDill:

  1. Understand that abuse is wrong. Every woman deserves to be treated kindly and gently. Because abuse is wrong, an abused woman must learn to say, "Stop, I won't tolerate this. I won't take it anymore."

  2. Find someone to talk to about what is going on.

  3. You must go, along with your confidant if need be, and make a police report regarding the physical violence.

  4. Call the pastor of your church—if he hasn't been told about your situation—and make an appointment to talk to him.

  5. Separate yourself from the abuse so that you can analyze what abuse is, how it began, and how you have become a captured part of the pattern.

6. Get individual and family therapy.

7. Avoid the quick-fix miracle ("I've changed—take me back!").

• "Scripture tells us 'Woman is the glory of the man' (1 Corinthians 11:7 [KJV]). She is not a doormat, a victim or a possession."

—Florence Littauer, *Taking Charge of Your Life*

Fourteen

Building a
Support System

*I*f self-pity were a virtue, I would win the title of Most Virtuous, hands down. There I sat, in my usual place at church: front row, middle section, second seat from the aisle. That's been my favorite place for more than twenty years, in whichever church I happen to attend.

That day I wore my most pitiful face and had planned to weep uncontrollably throughout the service. After all (sniff, sniff), I was Alone.

The praise team led the congregation in "Joy to the World," while I merely mouthed the words. *Ha!* I thought, *there is no joy in my world. After all (sniff, sniff), I'm Alone.*

Then God had to go and ruin my perfectly good bout of self-pity. A woman I barely knew came over and sat next to me. She leaned over and whispered, "I'm here alone too. How about if we sit together?"

Her gesture reminded me of a similar encounter with Terry, a woman who befriended me when I was a brand-new Christian. She too came to church alone, and she sought me out my first few weeks at First Baptist Church in Portland, Maine. She and I both had small children, and since we lived near each other, we spent nearly every day together for two years, searching the Scriptures and praying for one another until I moved away.

When I was with Terry, I was no longer alone. She understood— really, truly, completely understood. When I blew it and chased Barry around the house, nagging at him to "just come to church once and I promise I won't ask you again," she understood my tears of anger, remorse, and frustration. Since I was a new Christian (and therefore overly eager to push my faith on my dear husband), just knowing she understood made a hard situation bearable.

Since then, everywhere we've lived, the Lord has graciously provided a Terry: a like-minded woman to be my friend and support—and for me to be hers.

Friend, whether you're a new Christian—especially if you're new— or whether you've been unequally yoked for years, you need to find a Terry. It's not difficult either, since churches are filled with women who come to church alone. Just look around.

However, before you begin your relationship, keep in mind these guidelines:

- **Keep from gossiping.** No swapping "My husband's a bigger jerk than yours" stories. (Go back and read chapter 7.) Your relationship needs to be one of building up, not tearing down. Agree on this from the beginning and keep each other accountable.

- **Keep your priorities.** As sweet as it might be to find someone with whom you can be yourself, your primary earthly relationship is to be with your husband and your children. Watch your time together so you can get your home duties done properly (and not haphazardly or halfheartedly). Also, guard your heart, that your friendship doesn't become a stronghold or an idol in your life. It should never be your ultimate source of comfort and encouragement. That role belongs to God alone.

- **Keep it purposeful.** If the thought of starting an open-ended friendship sounds intimidating, try meeting once a week to go through a Bible study booklet together, perhaps one on marriage or one of the books of the Bible. Then, if the two of you "click," you can continue the friendship. If not, you've at least met another Christian and got into the Word of God with another believer.

- **Keep praying.** When you do find that soul connection with someone, strengthen each other by praying with and for each other. Pray through Scripture together. Pray for each other's husband. Sometimes it gets discouraging praying for your own husband, especially if you aren't seeing any progress or changes. It's often easier to pray for someone else.

- **Keep yourself from envy.** Be prepared that your friend's husband might turn to Christ quickly and yours may not. When that happens, believe me, it's so tempting to be envious. The thoughts of "But I've been waiting and praying longer!" will be right there to drive a wedge between the two of you. Keep in mind that God knows what he's doing. And he does all things well.

- **Keep it Christ-centered.** This doesn't mean you can't talk about politics or the weather, but stay mindful of who and whose you are. You are daughters of God. That means your advice to each other needs to be biblical. Forget about what you heard on *Oprah*. Only Jesus has the words of eternal life.

More One-on-One Support

Another valuable one-on-one support person to help you keep your focus is what many churches call a "Titus 2" woman: a mature Christian woman who is grounded in her faith. Taken from the book of Titus, this woman is instructed to "train the younger women to love their husbands and children, to be self-controlled and pure, to be busy at home, to be kind, and to be subject to their husbands, so that no one will malign the word of God" (Titus 2:4-5).

Sometimes this is a woman who lived a spiritually unequal life at one time and whose husband came to faith in Christ. A "been there" woman who knows your struggles and has seen God answer her prayers. Or maybe it's another unequally yoked woman who has learned to be content and has found freedom to be herself even in her situation.

As for me, God has placed dozens of godly Titus 2 women in my life. These older women consider me to be a daughter and send me notes and e-mails to say they're praying for my family and me. Over the years they've offered their shoulders to cry on and their assurance that God is still on his throne.

If you can find a godly older woman who will walk beside you, count yourself richly blessed. "Who can find a virtuous woman?" asks the writer of Proverbs. "For her price is far above rubies" (Proverbs 31:10, KJV).

We Are Family

In my church we don't call each other "Brother So-and-So" or "Sister Whoever," but our pastor has always emphasized that we are, indeed, brothers and sisters—children in God's family. When he talks about being a family he says, "Brothers and sisters, none of us walks to heaven alone. We walk together—as a family."

The apostle Paul told the Ephesians that we're "no longer foreigners and aliens, but fellow citizens with God's people and members of God's household" (Ephesians 2:19). In my church, when someone stands up for membership, all members stand with him or her as if to say, "Your burdens are my burdens; your needs I will help fill. Your children are my children, and we will help each other raise them in the Lord."

We eat together, laugh together, sit by each other's hospital beds, and stand by the grave sites of each other's loved ones. It's as a church should be. We are a family.

Ideally, a church family offers respite and care for its weariest members. Sadly, a common complaint among married women who go to church alone is feeling like they don't fit anywhere. Sunday school classes are generally designed for couples *or* singles—and they are neither. It's like churches don't know what to do with the "spiritually single." It's an anomaly. Square pegs in round holes.

I hope one of the churches in my area is typical of those in your area. If so, then the family of God is waking up to the needs of women who come to church alone. They've recently started a "Moms Without Partners" Sunday school class for married and unmarried moms. After only a few weeks of meeting together, the women agreed that they finally felt they had a place in the church, a place where they didn't feel like a failure just because they don't have a husband by their side.

How can you find support from your church? First of all, let someone know who you are! And don't consider yourself a bother or a burden. We're all bothers and burdens—that's what a family is all about.

Go to your pastor or an elder or women's ministry leader, and be honest about your needs and struggles. Put your name on the prayer chain. Have the men pray for your husband at their Saturday prayer breakfast.

If you have the opportunity, join a small group at your church, especially if your church is large. Ideally, they're structured as mini-churches within the bigger church and offer a true sense of family because of their small size. The healthiest small groups include members of all ages and stages of life, and they meet for a combination of fellowship, prayer, and Bible study. With a mixed group, no one feels isolated or like an "odd man out."

Unfortunately, many small groups meet at night when it's difficult to be away from home. Again, your priority needs to be your husband. I once belonged to a group that met every other Tuesday night. First we would eat dinner together, then we would have a Bible study. As much as I wanted to be with these people, as soon as I got in my car, I felt ripped in half. If I did go, I thought about Barry at home and felt I should be with him—even though he never gave me a hard time for going. Once I decided my place was with him, it was as if a tremendous weight had been lifted from me.

Meanwhile, the group kept me in their prayers and still considered me part of their family. Knowing that kept me encouraged.

If an evening group is out of the question for you, too, another option is to join a group that meets during the day, such as MOPS (Mothers of PreSchoolers) or Bible Study Fellowship. Or form a prayer or Bible study group at your workplace during your lunch break. Do what you can to find support within the body of Christ.

Other support options:

- Regularly visit Christian bookstores, and make friends with the people behind the counter.

- Read encouraging books to strengthen your faith.

- Familiarize yourself with your local Christian radio station, which is often used as a community "information central," with lots of resource materials and networking connections.

- Prayerfully and carefully find fellowship on the Web through e-mail lists or Christian women's chat rooms. (See the appendix at the end of this book for references and Web addresses.) As I write this, I know of several e-mail lists devoted to encouraging women in spiritually mismatched marriages, including one for Christian women married to Muslim men.

The body of Christ was designed to be interdependent. "In Christ we who are many form one body, and each member belongs to all the others" (Romans 12:5), wrote the apostle Paul to the Roman church. God has not called anyone to go through this journey alone. We go together. We go as a family. We hold each other up, rejoice with those who rejoice, weep with those who weep, and bear one another's burdens.

I pray you'll find someone to help you bear yours.

THINK ON THESE THINGS

- **Think** about the people in your life whose support you find valuable in your role as a wife who feels alone in her faith. Name some of the most helpful ways they've shown support.

- **Study** what the Bible says about friendship.
  Proverbs 17:17
  Proverbs 27:6,9,17
  Ecclesiastes 4:9-10

Galatians 6:2

Philippians 2:19-22

Who are the people in your life who meet these qualifications?

- **Apply** these scriptures to the role of other Christians in your life as well as to your role as a support person for others.

  Acts 2:42-47

  Acts 12:5

  1 Corinthians 12:12-27

  Ephesians 2:19-22

  Ephesians 4:16

  How well is your church meeting your needs? What are you doing or what can you do to meet the needs of others?

- **Consider** the three friends everyone needs: a mentor, a peer, and someone to mentor. Who are your three friends? If you're missing one in any category, ask the Lord to enlarge your circle. Each friend will help you grow to your fullest potential in Christ.

- "Friendship is born at that moment when one person says to another, 'What! You too? I thought I was the only one.'"

  —C. S. Lewis

Fifteen

And in the Days to Come...Hope

*M*aybe you wore white lace, with your hair done in a French braid. You chose your dearest friends as your bridesmaids, and together you chose the most exquisite shade of salmon pink for their gowns.

Maybe you rushed to the courthouse for a quick lunch-hour wedding. Maybe you stood in your mother's living room and exchanged vows before a justice of the peace. Maybe afterward you all went out to dinner or ate store-bought cake on paper plates.

Maybe it was your second or third marriage. Maybe you cried because you knew it was a mistake, but you went through with it anyway.

Whatever the circumstances, you took your beloved's hand and nervously recited your vows. You kissed. You laughed. You cried.

The two of you went off together with dreams of happily ever after, certain beyond certainty that nothing could or would ever separate "what God hath joined together."

But something—Someone—did.

This Someone entered your world and revealed to you that he is your true Husband. Then he dressed you in a wedding gown whiter than the whitest linen. You felt virginal again. And alive!

He kissed you with grace and vowed never to leave you or forsake you. And you longed to go and be with him.

You tried to explain your true Husband to your other husband, the one at home who plays on the computer and likes crumbled potato chips in his tomato soup. You thought for sure he would understand, but he didn't. He wouldn't. He couldn't.

Then it gripped you: *My life, my marriage, my family will never be the same again.*

So you continue to replay your mental wedding video of the Bridegroom standing at the altar with his Father. His face is radiant with joy at the sight of you proceeding down the aisle toward him, a crowd of witnesses urging you onward.

"My true Husband," you whisper to yourself. With him you are complete. With him you are utterly accepted, cherished, free. His love enfolds you like a fur coat, a warm quilt, the finest silk.

But then the husband playing on the computer in the other room asks you if he has any clean socks. Maybe you smile because you love the feel of his scratchy, unshaven face in the morning. Maybe you can't stand his touch. Maybe you feel nothing toward him.

Maybe you ache inside because both of your dreams of happily ever after were interrupted by Someone else—and you can't help thinking it's all your fault.

You wonder what the outcome will be. You wonder if you'll always feel torn between these two husbands…if you'll always feel rejected and misunderstood…if you'll ever truly find contentment and peace. Hope and joy.

You just want to laugh again! Throw your head back and roar from your belly—and mean it too.

Gifts from the Bridegroom

Let's go back to your wedding day. Maybe your beloved placed a locket around your neck or presented you with a bracelet. Maybe he didn't have much money, but because he knew how much you like bears or daisies or the color blue, he slipped a token out of his pocket and held it out with trembling fingers. He cupped your face in his hands and declared, "You know I'd buy you the moon if I could."

You knew he would too.

Maybe he promised you other gifts later on. "We'll build a life together. We'll have lots of children, maybe a dog. We'll have a house—and grandkids. Just me and you."

You still want those gifts. You want to enjoy them with the one who promised them to you. After all, he's your husband…

Now let's go back to your other wedding day, to your true Husband. He, too, promised you gifts. Only you're not so sure he gave you the ones he promised.

Or maybe you just failed to recognize them.

He promised patience and endurance. "God grows patience in our lives as we see his great patience with us," writes Bill Hybels in *Character: Reclaiming Six Endangered Qualities.* "When we picture how long-suffering and patient God has been with us it seems to just melt away our impatience. God slowly softens our hard hearts and quietly replaces them with an attitude of tolerance, understanding and forbearance."

The psalmist wrote, "The LORD is compassionate and gracious, slow to anger, abounding in love" (Psalm 103:8). Hybels adds, when we remember God's patience with us and with all who are still far from him and even running away, he calls us to share in the same patience God shows.

To do that, the Lord sends us gifts: a husband who is disinterested or even antagonistic toward spiritual things. Differences in temperament. Sickness. Diversity of opinions. Crisis. He places us within a marriage that sometimes becomes like sandpaper, an abrasive irritant, which eventually smoothes our rough edges. He sends trials to temper us and long periods of waiting, which force us to see that we wait, not for a husband to change, but for the Lord himself.

In her book *When I Prayed for Patience...God Let Me Have It!* Jeanne Zornes writes, "The hardest part of waiting is 'just before.' Just before you see the answer. Just before you're ready to give up. Just before it all breaks open, and you understand." Yet God tells us to wait—to wait for him.

And as we wait, our patience grows. Our groanings for relief grow softer and less frequent. We are stilled because we know that he is God. To whom else would we go? He alone has the words of eternal life. He promised to give us patience, and he has. And he does.

He promised contentment. You think you know what it will take to make you content. *Just change my husband's heart, Lord! Make him a Christian and then lead him to be a Sunday school teacher—and make it so he'll want to invite the neighbors over. And maybe you could nudge him to sing in the choir! I'll join too, and we can sing together.*

But when that doesn't happen right away, you bring your request down a notch. *Okay, Lord, just make him a Christian, and I'll be content with regular church and Sunday school attendance, midweek small group Bible study, and maybe choir.* The truth is, as long as you have a condition attached to your contentment ("Just make him a Christian!"), you'll never be content.

But that's okay, because God will teach you what true contentment is. Just look at the apostle Paul. He penned his famous "I have learned the secret of being content in any and every situation" while he was in prison and chained up. His secret? He discovered he can do all things through Christ who gives him the strength (Philippians 4:12-13).

When you reach the place where you stop your bargaining and put away your wish list, when you still your soul and are glad as you recount all that God has given you and not what he hasn't, then you will have learned the secret of contentment. "If God wants you in the place you are in right now, then there are no greener pastures," says author Stormie Omartian.

He hasn't forsaken you; he never says, "Oops." He hasn't withheld any good gifts (Psalm 84:11) and will complete everything he's started (Philippians 1:6). And he'll meet all your needs (Philippians 4:19).

It's enough. *He's* enough, he really is. So let go of your wish list and ask the Lord to teach you to be content. I promise you he will.

He promised comfort. I don't know how he does it, only that he does. The Bible calls it sufficient grace. We think we'll die of loneliness. We're misunderstood. Rejected. We think we can't go on a single moment longer...and then God comes to us.

Sometimes he comes disguised as another person with arms that wrap around us in a hug—even our husband. Sometimes he comes as a word. "I will never leave you or forsake you." Sometimes he comes as an image, such as a sunrise over a lake or a breeze blowing through the trees. Sometimes in the midst of our turmoil and confusion he simply invades with his Spirit and lifts us and sets our own spirit soaring. He doesn't change our situation, but he changes us. He comforts us. And he always gives us more than enough so we can pass it on to others who need comforting too.

I'll let you in on a secret: The more comfort you give away, the more you receive. The more you tell of God's promises and repeat your stories of his sufficient grace in times of greatest need, the greater your comfort.

When you remind others of God's amazing grace, you also remind yourself and your faith grows.

Playwright Thornton Wilder once wrote, "In Love's service, only the wounded can serve." God allows heartache and then offers his comfort so we will have compassion for the heartache of others. Only those who know the chasm of a spiritually unequal marriage and the comfort God gives can truly comfort others in the same situation. To say, "I know how you feel" and truly know—it's one of the greatest gifts we can give one another.

He promised purpose. As the prophet Jeremiah wrote, "'For I know the plans I have for you,' declares the LORD, 'plans to prosper you and not to harm you, plans to give you hope and a future'" (Jeremiah 29:11). The apostle Paul reminds us that we are God's workmanship and that he's already prepared good works for us to do.

You may think you can't serve the Lord where you are, that your unequal yoke is chafing at your neck and that your husband is holding you back. You may think ministry means teaching Sunday school or serving on committees. You may think you have to wait for your husband to come to faith before you can serve. Forgive me for being blunt, but if that's what you think, you're wrong. God is far too creative—not to mention powerful—to be so limited.

According to the Westminster Confession of Faith, the chief end of man is to glorify God and enjoy him forever. If he has created us, if he has called us, if he has equipped us, if he has said he has already prepared good works for us to do, then surely he's able to direct us to discover them!

I love the theme song to the Disney *Aladdin* movie, in which Aladdin sings to the princess about a whole new world that he wants to show her. I especially love the part when he sings, "Don't you dare close your eyes—it gets better." I always think that's what Jesus sings to us. That he's created this whole new world for us to discover, including his purpose for us as women and as wives. So don't you dare close your eyes! It gets better.

He promised laughter. Actually, he promised joy—his joy, which is our strength (Nehemiah 8:10). But with joy comes laughter. Marjorie Holmes once wrote, "The world is so full of anguish; life itself sometimes seems so grim. Thank you [Lord] that in your vast understanding you gave us laughter to make us forget, to restore our wounded spirits, brighten the journey, lighten the load."

I love the absurdity of life. As I write this, I have the entire contents of a feather pillow inside my washing machine, dryer, and vacuum cleaner. I have teeny bird feathers up my nose and in my hair. I spent the greater part of this afternoon discovering that, yes, you can indeed wash feather pillows in the washing machine. However, stapling a rip in the fabric won't keep the feathers from escaping.

I realize this has nothing to do with being married to an unbeliever, but the whole incident made me laugh so hard I cried. That's not unusual. Lots of people do that. But only those who belong to Christ can cry until they laugh. That's *joy.*

In *My Utmost for His Highest,* Oswald Chambers wrote, "The saint is hilarious when crushed with difficulties because the thing is so ludicrously impossible to anyone but God." When your husband is cold, when he snaps and barks, when you want to reach out to him but all your best efforts are rebuffed, when you want to pound on God's chest—and cuss—when all you can do is lie crumpled in a heap on the floor, sobbing...that's when the laughter comes. Not because life is funny, but because things are so utterly out of your control that all you can do is laugh. *I give up, Lord! I surrender. You're God—I'm not.*

That's when God steps in and reveals himself in a fresh and personal way, and it fills you with joy...and that's when you laugh.

He promised hope. Regarding the subject of hope, G. K. Chesterton said, "Hope means hoping when things are hopeless, or it is no virtue at all.... As long as matters are really hopeful, hope is mere flattery or platitude; it is only when everything is hopeless that hope begins to be a strength."

Hope isn't hope if you can see the thing you hope for. Instead, hope scratches its head and says, "This thing will never fly"—and it does.

The book of Acts records a story of a group of the Lord's disciples praying for Peter, who was in prison. An angel came to his prison cell and helped him escape. When he went to the house where the people were praying for him, even when a servant girl announced that Peter was at the door, they told her she was crazy. Even though they prayed, they secretly thought it was hopeless.

God seems to work best when things appear bleakest. He promises a decrepit old man that he will father nations—and he does. He tells a virgin she will bear a child—and she does. He waits until a body is good and dead—then raises it back to eternal life.

He tells a woman to respect and honor her husband and never give up hope.

The old man, Abraham, hoped; so did his old wife, Sarah. King David hoped, even when he was being hunted down by a crazy Saul. Jonah hoped from inside the belly of a fish. Paul hoped from inside a prison. They hoped because they knew God was and is a God of hope, who fills his people "with all joy and peace as [they] trust in him, so that [they] may overflow with hope by the power of the Holy Spirit" (Romans 15:13).

The writer of Hebrews tells us after Abraham waited patiently, he received what God had promised. "God did this so that...we who have fled to take hold of the hope offered to us may be greatly encouraged. We have this hope as an anchor for the soul, firm and secure" (Hebrews 6:18-19).

The God of hope gives us an anchor of hope to keep us moored to him. He holds us. He grips us tightly. He's stable and sure, kind and almighty. If we have given our lives to the Lord, he's in control of everything that pertains to us. That's our hope—and hope is what will see us through to the end.

With This Ring

Let's go back one last time to your wedding day. Maybe your husband—the one who clips his toenails in the living room—placed a plain gold band on your finger. Maybe you didn't have much money for a ring at the time, so you only paid twenty-five dollars for the one you're wearing, and after all these years, it has lost its luster. It's beat up, misshapen. Lopsided. *Kinda like my life,* you think.

You'd like a new ring, but…

But what you really want is a diamond. You've never said anything to your husband—he has enough to worry about, with dental bills and needing a new roof and all. So you tuck the thought of a diamond ring away and go on with your life.

Years go by. Hard years. Good years. Blah years. You and your husband grow close, move apart, tiptoe around as if on eggshells, dance until dawn. Then one day you find a ring box in the glove compartment of his car. It just tumbles out at your feet.

Your husband smiles and says, "That's for you."

It's a diamond ring, and as you take off your old, lopsided gold band and slip on the most exquisite piece of jewelry you've ever seen, you can't believe how perfectly it fits your finger. You squeal with delight, or maybe you cry, and your husband grins as you hug his neck.

You hold your hand out *just so* until the diamond catches a beam of light and scatters it into a burst of colors. As you watch the way the diamond sparkles and shines, your thoughts are drawn to your true Husband, and you realize the ring is really a gift from him. It's his way of saying, "I've taken something marred and misshapen and turned it into something precious and priceless."

Then he gives you a geology lesson and tells you how a diamond is formed: Picture the interior structure of the Earth's three layers: the core, mantle, and crust. A diamond starts out as a hunk of carbon, one of the most common elements in creation—nothing more than a lump of coal—deep within the mantle of the Earth.

It's only under extreme heat and intense pressure that the carbon becomes crystallized into a diamond. But the process doesn't stop there. The only way the diamond reaches the Earth's crust is through molten rock, which explodes from a volcano. It's the *process* that turns the common and ordinary into the toughest and most precious gem there is.

You ponder that awhile and try to decipher its meaning. You ask, "Lord, are you saying you're changing my marriage into something precious like this ring?"

But he doesn't answer.

So you think some more. You sit out on your front porch and watch the cars drive by and feel the wind blow through your hair. You think about hunks of coal and extreme heat and intense pressure...and the way a diamond can catch a single beam of light and scatter it in a dozen directions.

That's when you realize that your marriage may never be a diamond but that you are and always will be.

That's our hope.

That God takes us through the heat and the pressure until we emerge strong and durable, brilliant reflectors of light. His light.

I'd love to end this book by promising "Just follow these principles, and you can love your husband into God's kingdom in thirty days or your money back." I can't even promise that if it were possible to do everything right, your marriage would be heaven on earth. I can't even guarantee my own marriage will survive.

But I will survive, and so will you.

We're God's diamonds.

One Final Word from Your True Husband

Through the prophet Isaiah, the Lord says:

> "Do not be afraid; you will not suffer shame.
>> Do not fear disgrace; you will not be humiliated.
> You will forget the shame of your youth
>> and remember no more the reproach of your widowhood.
> For your Maker is your husband—
>> the LORD Almighty is his name—
> the Holy One of Israel is your Redeemer;
>> he is called the God of all the earth.
> The LORD will call you back
>> as if you were a wife deserted and distressed in spirit—
> a wife who married young,
>> only to be rejected," says your God. (Isaiah 54:4-6)

We may not know the future, but of this we can be sure: We know the One who called us is faithful. He comforts us and gives us patience, contentment, and joy. He gives us a purpose...and hope. He has placed us within our marriages and has given us all we need that he might be glorified and that we might shine like the diamonds we are.

—————— ⟨⟩ ——————

THINK ON THESE THINGS

- **Think** about getting a call from your best friend saying, "I have a present for you—I'll be right over." How would you feel? What would be your thoughts?

- **Study** Romans 8. Note every verse that gives you a reason to hope or be encouraged. After this exercise, think about how God feels toward you as his child. Write down your thoughts. According to Romans 8, how does God feel about your marriage?

- **Apply** what you've discovered in Romans 8 by using your own words to define the word "hope." Now look up these additional scriptures about hope to see how close your definition comes to what God's Word says:
  Psalm 25:3
  Isaiah 49:23
  Jeremiah 31:16-17
  Romans 4:18
  Romans 5:2-5
  Romans 15:13
  Ephesians 1:18
  Colossians 1:27
  Hebrews 11:1
  1 Peter 1:21
  Choose one of these verses, memorize it, and recite it to yourself often. How does it speak to your heart regarding your marriage?

• **Consider** other gifts and demonstrations of grace and mercy God has given you. Be specific—and be sure to tell other women with unbelieving husbands. You'll be blessed when you do.

• "If…you started out all wrong, who's to say God can't use your relationship to bless not only your lives but future generations as well? Who's to say your marriage hasn't been in the plan of God from eternity past? All of heaven is on your side. Christ himself wants you to succeed.… May the God of all hope be with you both."

—Bob Moeller, *For Better, for Worse, for Keeps*

appendix of resources

National Child Abuse Hotline
1-800-422-4453

National Council on Alcoholism
1-800-NCA-CALL (622-2255)

National Domestic Violence Hotline
Call toll-free 24 hours 1-800-799-SAFE (7233)
For hearing-impaired call 1-800-572-SAFE (7233)

To Find a Counselor in Your Area
Call your local church for a referral or look in the yellow pages of your telephone book under:

> Marriage and Family Counseling
>
> Mental Health Services
>
> Psychologists

For Further Reading

Barnes, Bob. *What Makes a Man Feel Loved.* Eugene, Oreg.: Harvest House, 1998.

Chapman, Gary. *The Five Love Languages.* Chicago, Ill.: Northfield Publishing, 1995.

Dillow, Linda, and Lorraine Pintus. *Intimate Issues.* Colorado Springs, Colo.: WaterBrook, 1999.

Dobson, James. *Love Must Be Tough.* Waco, Tex.: Word, 1983.

LaHaye, Tim, and Beverly LaHaye. *The Act of Marriage.* Grand Rapids, Mich.: Zondervan, 1998.

McDill, S. R., and Linda McDill. *Dangerous Marriage: Breaking the Cycle of Domestic Violence.* Grand Rapids, Mich.: Spire, 1991.

Means, Marsha. *Living with Your Husband's Secret Wars.* Grand Rapids, Mich.: Revell, 1999. (for help with a husband's pornography addiction)

Moeller, Robert. *For Better, for Worse, for Keeps.* Sisters, Oreg.: Multnomah, 1993.

Parrott, Les, and Leslie Parrott. *When Bad Things Happen to Good Marriages: How to Stay Together When Life Pulls You Apart.* Grand Rapids, Mich.: Zondervan, 2001.

Strobel, Lee. *Inside the Mind of Unchurched Harry and Mary.* Grand Rapids, Mich.: Zondervan, 1993.

Wright, H. Norman. *What Men Want.* Ventura, Calif.: Regal, 1996.

For Internet Support

New Life Partners is a Christian-based support group for women whose husbands are caught in the web of sexual addiction. Here you will find sharing, caring, love, hope, and prayer to help you daily work out the Lord's plan for your life. *http://groups.yahoo.com/group/newlifepartners*

Hope in a House Divided is a forum for women who are desiring to live by God's principles in homes divided by emotional or physical detachment, an unbelieving or uncommitted husband, separation, or divorce. *www.house-of-hope.net*

Christianitytoday.com offers prayer message boards and prayer chat rooms, plus lots of online reading. Visit them at *www.christianitytoday.com.*

Won Without a Word offers a newsletter, marriage links, a poet's corner, and an e-mail group for Christian women with unsaved husbands. *www.netutah.com/wonwithoutaword*

about the author

As a freelance writer since 1989, Nancy Kennedy has written several books, including *Prayers God Always Answers* and *Move Over, Victoria—I Know the Real Secret!* Her work has also appeared in *Reader's Digest, Christian Parenting Today, Today's Christian Woman, Virtue, Marriage Partnership, Parents of Teenagers, Moody Magazine, Aspire,* and many other publications.

Currently she's a feature writer, editor, and columnist for her local daily paper, the *Citrus County Chronicle.* Her religion page features have won three First Place Excellence in Religion Writing awards from the Florida Press Club.

You can read her weekly column, "Grace Notes," through the *Citrus County Chronicle*'s online site at www.chronicleonline.com. To access it, click on "Features."

You can contact Nancy Kennedy in care of Seven Rivers Presbyterian Church, 4221 W. Gulf-to-Lake Hwy, Lecanto, FL 34461.

73940